Cambridge Elements ≡

Elements in Corpus Linguistics
edited by
Susan Hunston
University of Birmingham

THE IMPACT OF EVERYDAY LANGUAGE CHANGE ON THE PRACTICES OF VISUAL ARTISTS

Darryl Hocking
Auckland University of Technology

CAMBRIDGE
UNIVERSITY PRESS

CAMBRIDGE
UNIVERSITY PRESS

University Printing House, Cambridge CB2 8BS, United Kingdom

One Liberty Plaza, 20th Floor, New York, NY 10006, USA

477 Williamstown Road, Port Melbourne, VIC 3207, Australia

314–321, 3rd Floor, Plot 3, Splendor Forum, Jasola District Centre,
New Delhi – 110025, India

103 Penang Road, #05–06/07, Visioncrest Commercial, Singapore 238467

Cambridge University Press is part of the University of Cambridge.

It furthers the University's mission by disseminating knowledge in the pursuit of
education, learning, and research at the highest international levels of excellence.

www.cambridge.org
Information on this title: www.cambridge.org/9781009225731
DOI: 10.1017/9781108909693

First published 2022

A catalogue record for this publication is available from the British Library.

ISBN 978-1-009-22573-1 Paperback
ISSN 2632-8097 (online)
ISSN 2632-8089 (print)

The Impact of Everyday Language Change on the Practices of Visual Artists

Elements in Corpus Linguistics

DOI: 10.1017/9781108909693
First published online: April 2022

Darryl Hocking
Auckland University of Technology

Author for correspondence: Darryl Hocking, dhocking@aut.ac.nz

Abstract: The practices of visual artists can never be decontextualised from language. First, artists are constantly in dialogue with their peers, dealers, critics and audiences about their creative activities and these interactions impact on the work they produce. Second, artists' conceptualisations of what artistic practice encompasses are always shaped by wider social discourses. These discourses, however, and their manifestation in the language of everyday life are subject to continual change and potentially reshape the way that artists conceptualise their practices. Using a 235,000-word diachronic corpus developed from artists' interviews and statements, this Element investigates shifts in artists' use of language to conceptualise their art practice from 1950 to 2019. It then compares these shifts to see if they align with changes in the wider English lexicon and whether there might be a relationship between everyday language change and the aesthetic and conceptual developments that take place in the art world.

Keywords: visual art, corpus analysis, diachronic corpus analysis, discourse analysis, art and language

ISBNs: 9781009225731 (PB), 9781108909693 (OC)
ISSNs: 2632-8097 (online), 2632-8089 (print)

Contents

1 Introduction

This Element investigates diachronic shifts in the way that contemporary artists in English-speaking contexts have used language to conceptualise their art practice from 1950 to 2019. It then compares these shifts to see whether they align with diachronic changes in the wider English lexicon. The aim is to establish whether there is some relationship between the shifts in everyday language use and the aesthetic and conceptual developments that take place over time in the art world. In carrying out these objectives, the Element also provides a case study for the use of corpus analysis to examine connections between the specialist languages that mediate the practices of professional, institutional or cultural communities and the more general language use of their wider contexts.

To achieve its aims, the Element first examines a 235,000-word diachronic corpus developed from artists' interviews and statements from 1950 until 2019. This is referred to as the Artists' Language Corpus (hereafter, ALC). The first stage of the study examines the ALC to identify significant trends that have occurred in the way that artists represented by the corpus have used language to conceptualise their creative practices. As an example, the Element will show that, in the early twentieth century, an artist's practice frequently involved what they conceptualised as an attempt to *solve a problem*, however, this creative motivation waned as the twentieth century progressed and other discursive constructions began to motivate creative practice, such as depicting the *essence of memory*. Indeed, following the discourse theories of Fairclough (1992), as well as Phillips and Hardy (2002), who, among others, view our social lives, identities and practices as being brought into play by language, rather than language being a simple reflection of that which already exists, this Element takes the view that the language used by artists to describe their work has an important constitutive function. That is, if at a particular point in time art practice is widely conceptualised through the language of *solving a problem*, then this discursive understanding of art will tend to motivate the type of work that is produced by artists at that particular time.

Given this understanding, it is also very likely that the specific language used by artists to conceptualise their practices tends to emerge from a wider social and historical context. As such, the second stage of this Element seeks to establish whether changes in the wider lexicon might exhibit a relationship with the changes that were found to occur over time in the ALC. To achieve this, the Element examines whether the findings from the first stage of the analysis statistically correlate with language shifts in the Corpus of Historical American English (COHA), one of the largest available diachronic corpora (Davis, 2010). Overall, the study draws on the corpus-analytical resources associated with Modern Diachronic Corpus Assisted Discourse Studies (Partington, 2010; Marchi, 2018), notably trend mapping and correlation, but it also involves tools, such as frequency, collocation and concordance analysis, often used for the corpus-based analysis of discourse (Baker, 2006).

Section 1.1 further establishes the belief underpinning this study that language is constitutive of creative practice and provides historical examples of the type of language used by artists to discursively conceptualise their creative practices. Section 1.2 provides a brief review of studies that examine the relationship between art and language, from Harris' (2003) historical study of artspeak in the western tradition, to Rule and Levine's (2012) critique of contemporary arts writing. Section 2 describes and justifies the methods, analytical procedures and statistical measures used throughout the Element. It also provides details about ALC, the specialised diachronic corpus developed for the Element. Section 3 uses corpus analytical tools to identify key diachronic trends found in the ALC. Findings are statistically supported and visualised using figures. Section 4 compares the trends identified in Section 3 with the diachronic reference corpus COHA, to evaluate whether shifts in the way visual artists have discursively conceptualised and legitimised their work throughout the past century align with those occurring in general language use. The section also further examines the occurrence in COHA of some of the lemmas identified as trending in the ALC in an attempt to account for their increasing or decreasing use by artists over time. Finally, Section 5 draws on the previous section to discuss the implications of the findings and consider whether artistic developments in contemporary art practice are in some way shaped by language shifts in the wider English lexicon.

1.1 The Role of Language in Contemporary Art Practice

The creative practices of contemporary visual artists can never be decontextualised from language. First, artists are constantly in dialogue with their peers, dealers, collectors, critics, audiences and acquaintances about their creative activities and these interactions continually impact on and shape the work that they produce. The prominent twentieth-century art dealer Daniel-Henry Kahnweiler, for example, identified the constant 'friendly conversations' between Pablo Picasso and George Braque as crucial to the important advances that took place in early twentieth-century painting (Kahnweiler, 1949: 6). In another example, the letters of the influential New Zealand dealer Peter McLeavy show that he would regularly visit his artists' studios as a way of controlling the quality and direction of their work; a process that he explicitly states would take place through talk (Trevelyan, 2013).

Second, artists' particular conceptualisations of what artistic practice encompasses is always subject to wider macro discourses.[1] One way that these conceptualisations are constituted is through the published writings of influential individuals. A notable example is the Renaissance architect Alberti's 1485 treatise in which *beauty* was first proposed as the highest ideal of art; a concept that would go on to dominate European art practice for three centuries (Harris, 2003). A more recent example, and one influential to the practices of contemporary artists in the second half of the twentieth century, is Sol LeWitt's 1967 essay, which argued that the idea informing an artwork was more important than its physical form (LeWitt, 1967). Although he personally rejected his influence (Ostrow, 2003), LeWitt was reproducing prior discourses about the primacy of the idea in visual art by the seminal artist Marcel Duchamp. In a 1946 interview, for instance, Duchamp stated that 'I wanted to get away from the physical aspect of painting. I was much more interested in recreating ideas in painting' (Sweeney, 1946).

The language found in the statements, manifestos, essays or interviews of artists throughout time can therefore provide useful information about the types of discourses that artists draw on to conceptualise and motivate their creative practices. For example, in the early modernist period, artists tended to discursively conceptualise their work as a *study* and were motivated by the notion of their practice being an educational pursuit. As a result, artists would employ the resources of their creative practice to carry out repeated detailed *studies* of a landscape, a bowl of fruit or the human figure to *learn* about its form and how to represent its unique essence. In his letters to Émile Bernard, for example, the French modernist Paul Cézanne states that 'the painter should devote himself completely to the study [l'étude] of nature, and try to produce paintings that will be an education [enseignement]' (Cezanne, 1904, cited in Danchev, 2013: 339). He conceptualised this process as a sustained personal endeavour due to its inherent complexity and believed that it transcended his predecessors' focus on technique, which he dismissed as 'formulas' (Cezanne, 1905, cited in Danchev, 2013: 353). An examination of the language used by Vincent Van Gogh in his letters indicates how he also discursively conceptualised his practice as a study. In an 1889 letter to his brother Theo, for example, he stated that: 'It's the *study*

---

[1] The use of the term 'discourses' here refers to the words, statements or ways of speaking that produce people's understanding of certain concepts, objects and practices (Fairclough, 1992). As will be discussed, an example is the way that some people (including some art critics) are influenced by certain historical discourses when they only perceive an artwork as legitimate if it exhibits what they refer to as 'artistic taste' or 'beauty'.

[l'étude] of the figure that *teaches* [apprendre] one to grasp the essential and simplify (Van Gogh 1889, cited in Jansen et al., 2009).

By the 1920s, contemporary artists began to conceptualise their work through the still ubiquitous nineteenth-century discourses of exploration and discovery (Hocking, 2018). These discourses, with their emphasis on the new and unknown, provided artists with an opportune vocabulary to facilitate the emergent creative processes that could represent the widespread industrial advances taking place in Europe at the time, as well as the novel experiences that these advances brought to everyday life. According to the art historian Efland (1990), this focus of art and design practice as exploration first appeared in the foundation programme of the innovative Bauhaus art school in Germany. As such, exploration discourses are repeatedly evident in both the texts produced by the Bauhaus and the subsequent descriptions of the Bauhaus programmes by its masters. For instance, in the Breviary for Bauhaus Members, Walter Gropius stated that the 'common creative source' of art and technology 'must be explored and rediscovered' (Gropius, 1924, cited in Stein 1980: 76), an allusion to an explorer's pursuit for the source of a river. Gropius later described the Bauhaus as 'preoccupied with exploring the territory' (Gropius 1965: 90) and Johnannes Itten referring to Bauhaus assignments on colour and texture suggested that 'a whole new world was discovered' (Itten, 1964: 147). Art as exploration discourses are still widely pervasive today and artists frequently characterise their creative practices as explorations in unknown countries, as exciting adventures or as continuous journeys. Importantly, by the late 1950s, with the wider emergence of a focus on the conceptual, the discourses of exploration and ideas merged. The practices of artists were increasingly motivated by the conceptualisation of their work as the exploration of ideas, concepts, issues or possibilities, as can be seen in LeWitt's 1967 manifesto where he stated that 'if the artist wishes to explore his idea thoroughly, then arbitrary or chance decisions would be kept to a minimum' (LeWitt, 1967: 80).

Since the 1970s, the increasing inclusion of visual art as a university discipline, and the related requirement to validate the emergence of a new studio-based culture within the university context, has resulted in the reconceptualisation of creative practice as research that produces new knowledge (Elkins, 2009). Elkins points out that this emergent research discourse in the creative arts arises from the standardisation of university policies; that is, art departments like other departments 'must endeavour to add to knowledge through new research' (p. 112). He states that a wealth of literature accompanying the institutionalisation of the visual arts studio has over time naturalised the art as research discourse and in doing so has hidden its institutionally motivated origins. Consequently, contemporary visual artists now frequently refer to their art making as 'research-based practice' or simply 'research'. In an interview, for instance, the artist-duo Gilbert and George described their artistic practice as 'always *research*, always continuing, non-stop' (The Talks, 2011: para. 38). Evident in this remark is the reproduction of the study discourse's entailment of persistence, seen decades earlier in Cézanne's conceptualisation of his practice as a 'never-ending' [incessant], life-long endeavour (Cezanne, 1904, cited in Danchev, 2013: 337). A more recent example of the research discourse is apparent in a comment by the contemporary artist Kameelah Janan Rasheed, who, in an interview in *Artforum*, stated that: 'I've stopped seeing myself primarily as an artist. I'm more of a learner who is trying to make her research and inquiries visible through an ecosystem of different media or experiments' (Halpert, 2019: para. 2). In this comment, Rasheed discursively reconceptualises her artistic practice as research, effectively a result of the experiments that she conducts. Furthermore, and again evoking the related study discourse, she also conceptualises herself as a learner.

To conclude this introductory section, two important points should be made. First, I would argue that the language of the discourses that conceptualise art over time becomes entrenched in the lexicon of contemporary artists as constitutive of the natural and therefore legitimate actions of art practice. For example, the action of 'exploring' some phenomenon through visual practice has gradually come to be understood as something that artists might legitimately do as art. At the same time, these discourses enable artists to rationalise their work to their audiences through the verbal texts they produce, in particular the artists' interview or the artists' statement. However, artists themselves are not always explicitly conscious of the discourses that motivate and ultimately legitimise their practices.

Second, the writings of Alberti or LeWitt, the thoughts of Duchamp, the values of Cézanne, or the beliefs underpinning art institutions – all of which have unquestionably informed subsequent creative practices – are themselves shaped by wider social discourses; discourses that, it could be argued, are often manifested in everyday language. For example, and referring specifically to the early twentieth-century conceptualisation of art as exploration, it is well documented that a 'culture of exploration' was prevalent throughout Europe in the late nineteenth century and that this became a central focus of literary, economic, religious, political, scientific and, notably, aesthetic life (e.g., Driver, 2001, 2004). The next section looks briefly at some of the published literature investigating the relationship between language and art practice, focussing in particular on the types of (often competing) discourses that shape the conceptualisation of artistic practice.

1.2 Literature Review

1.2.1 Roy Harris and Artspeak

Roy Harris' (2003) *The Necessity of Artspeak* provides one of the more comprehensive historical overviews of the role that language has played in the conceptualisation of art practice in the western tradition. His study begins by making the important point that given the evidence of myriad treatises and manuals of instruction produced by arts practitioners from the early Greek sculptors onwards, the arts in antiquity were fundamentally connected to literacy. That is, artistic knowledge, and the status it entailed, was not simply demonstrated through visual practice, but through the ability to theoretically explain the principles of artistic practice in writing. According to Harris, this connection between the verbal and the visual has had a profound effect on the western tradition of the arts; predominantly by giving precedent to theory over practice, but also by elevating the status of those arts that could be made verbally explicit over those which could be developed merely through tacit 'observation and imitation' (p. 23).

In light of this observation, Harris explains how certain discourses have shaped the conceptualisation of visual arts practice. A major example involves Plato's critique of poetry in *The Republic* (Book X), in which he defines oratory, painting and sculpture as simply nothing more than 'imitations' of nature. That is, Plato believed the objects produced by these arts were simply static illusions of the more complex reality that they were attempting to depict and that similarly the techniques exemplified in the written treatises and manuals of instruction were deficient representations of the writer's actual knowledge (see Harris, 2000). Plato's attack, however, is widely viewed as being motivated by his attempt to increase the status of his own discipline philosophy over poetry, the latter was, at the time, regarded as the most literate, and therefore most exalted, of the arts (see also Halliwell, 1988: 120). Nevertheless, the discursive relationship that Plato established between art and nature continued to have resonance throughout history. The philosopher Lucius Annaeus Seneca (4 BC–65 AD), for example, claimed that 'all art is but imitation of nature' (Seneca, trans. 1925: 445) in his *Moral Letters to Lucilius* (AD 65), and the Roman educator and rhetorician Quintilian (AD 35–100) stated in his influential text, *Instititutio Oratoria* (95AD), that 'in art no small portion of our task lies in imitation' (Quintilian, trans. 1939: 139).

Another important instance of language shaping changes in western visual arts practice, mentioned by Harris, involves the Renaissance architect Leon Battista Alberti. As mentioned earlier, Alberti believed that art should not only resemble nature but should also be beautiful. Alberti made this claim in his influential fifteenth-century treatise on architecture, *De Pictura* (1435), when he wrote that 'let him not only prefer the resemblance of things but also, and above all, beauty itself' (Alberti, trans. 2011: 78). He goes on to criticise a celebrated ancient painter, Demetrius, who he states, 'did not reach the maximum level of praise, because he was more careful in expressing resemblance than beauty' (p. 78). Harris (2003) argues that the conceptualisation of painting promoted by Alberti was 'to dominate European thinking in the arts for three centuries' (p. 46) and points out that even in 1929, the *Encyclopaedia Britannica* was continuing to state that 'the function of art is the creation of beauty' (*Encyclopaedia Britannica*, 14th ed., vol. 2, cited in Harris, 2003: 46).

Taking into account these and other historical examples, Harris states that 'writing about it [art] is as influential culturally as producing actual works of art'. He refers to language about art as 'artspeak' and argues that 'artspeak, far from passively reflecting the practice of artist, *begins to determine what practices shall be granted the status of arts*' (Harris, 2003: 28 [emphasis added]).

1.2.2 Contemporary and Competing Discourses

The language used to conceptualise art practice and provide artists with a textual catalyst for their practice in the late twenty-first century is often viewed as informed by French structuralist and post-structuralist theory (e.g., Foucault, Deleuze, Derrida) which was introduced to artists in the late 1970s (Kester, 2011; Lejeune, Mignon and Pirenne, 2013). According to Lejeune et al., this occurred because a number of journals at the time began translating and interrogating French thought into English with an experimentation of form and tone that resonated with artists looking to justify or enhance their practices. The French theoretical foci on areas such as intertextuality, deconstruction, subjectivity and language itself also worked to shift artists' work away from the types of traditional discourse of beauty, originality and artistic skill, as well as the materials and media that had previously dominated visual arts practice.

The emergence of these new discourses, however, often sits problematically alongside those of the past. Gillon's (2017) study of the published commentaries on the Turner Prize – the preeminent contemporary British art award – provides some useful insights into the often competing discourses that pervade the conceptualisation of contemporary arts practice. As Gillon points out, many of those who critique the validity of artworks nominated for the Turner Prize have, through expressions such as 'I could do that' (Gillon 2017: 22), constructed the works as lacking what they believe is a required level of beauty or technical skill. Those who defend such works, which, as mentioned, often involve new artistic media such as film-based art and installation art, suggest that although they fall outside the traditional disciplines they are nevertheless still 'extremely well crafted' (Gillon 2017: 23). Another defence seen in Gillon (2017) involves what I might refer to as a discourse of process, that is, the artwork lacking a perceived level of skill may instead be legitimised as the result of an intensive process of labour. The oppositional nature of contemporary art discourse is also evident in Roose, Roose and Daenekindt's (2018) analysis of the topics discussed in 6,965 articles published between 1991 and 2015 in the leading art magazine *Frieze*. They suggest that two prominent art discourses are apparent throughout these years of the publication. The first focusses on formal and aesthetic concerns and is shaped by the more traditional concepts such as originality, beauty and authenticity, while the second focusses on societal concerns and is shaped by concepts appropriated from traditionally non-artistic areas such as politics, philosophy, history and economics.

1.2.3 Discourses of Art Practice in Education

Competing discourses are also found in arts education. Banaji, Burn and Buckingham (2010), for example, using the term 'rhetorics', identify nine different discourses that shape education in the arts. These include the traditionalist creative genius rhetoric that views arts creativity as the special ability of certain highly educated or inspired individuals, an anti-elitist democratic and political rhetoric that focusses on creativity as the 'everyday cultural and symbolic practices of all human beings' (p. 69) and the economic imperative rhetoric whereby student creativity is linked to the creative industries and neoliberal economic programmes. Hocking (2018) has also examined the way that written and spoken communication facilitates creative practice in university arts education, showing that such communication is often shaped by a complex network of historically formed and intersecting discourses, including work, ideas, agency, motivation and identity. The discourse of work, for example, constructs creatively successful art practice in the studio as a habitual, routine-based and time-effective activity involving the ongoing production of multiple creative outputs. This discourse was seen as being reproduced in the studio tutors' utterances such as 'through the hard work the creativity comes out' (p. 77), or in design briefs stating that students must 'work quickly' and develop a 'good work habit' (p. 71). It is also often linked to the discourse of process, as mentioned earlier.

1.2.4 The Influence of Language on Interpretations of Art

The analysis of the way in which language is used to explain the work of art, predominantly through the genre of the explanatory text usually found alongside the artwork in an exhibition or online digitised collection, is a prominent focal area of research involving the relationship between language and visual arts practice. Blunden (2020), for instance, shows how the language of explanatory texts achieve their aim by first motivating the reader/viewer to focus on a particular feature of the artwork constructed as salient (i.e., *the white lilies*) and then adding to this feature further meanings that are not visible in the artwork (i.e., *symbolise purity and the annunciation*). She correctly claims that this type of relationship between the verbal and visual '"adds something more" to the looking' (p. 55). In another example, Cunningham (2019) statistically examined a corpus of 180 online explanatory texts from the collections of a number of online museums and found that they could be clustered into five different groups based on their particular use of linguistic features, including those employing highly descriptive and informative language to construct the artwork as a product and those using expansive and interpretative language to construct the artwork as a process. Using a corpus containing 160 artists' statements and the paintings to which they referred, which was created from four volumes of a prominent art magazine from 2002–3, Sullivan (2009) examined the different ways that representational and abstract artists conceptualise their work through metaphors of communication, such as *language, conversation, dialogue, translate* and *interpret*. In her corpus, for example, Sullivan noticed that *language* was used by eight representational artists and five abstract artists. She found that the representational artists used *language* to refer to either their methods or the inventory of objects (buildings, skyscrapers) used in their paintings, while for the abstract painters *language* consisted of sets of shapes and colours. Importantly, Sullivan found that representational artists viewed their work as metaphorically speaking to their audience, while abstract artists tended to enter into a metaphorical conversation with their materials.

Empirical studies have also investigated the impact of explanatory statements on the viewer's reception of the artwork. Specht (2010), for example, found that those who read an explanatory statement before viewing a work were ultimately more positive about the work, especially if the work was representational, while Temme (1992) found that the enjoyment of looking at paintings increased for most museum visitors when they were accompanied by written information. However, in contrast to Specht, this only occurred when the paintings were considered 'artistically ambiguous' (p. 35). Another area of research into writing associated with the visual arts involves the genre of the artists' statement. Hocking (2021), for example, analyses the rhetorical moves and related lexical features of the artists' statement, Lise (2013) and Adamson and Goddard (2012) discuss the emergence, history and function of the artists' statement, while Belshaw (2011) examines how artists use the statement to shape their unique artistic identities. Finally, Garrett-Petts and Nash (2008) argue that the artists' statement plays an important generative role in the artists' practice. These studies all provide further support for the claim that writing about art is constitutive of artistic production and reception.

1.2.5 Critiques of Artspeak

As the language used to conceptualise art practice continues to evolve, those accustomed to prior, more established art discourses are often critical of the new ways that contemporary art is discursively framed. Kester (2011), for example, views the use of French theoretical texts as a catalyst for artistic work as superficial. He describes the practice as a 'liturgical relationship to theory', which he states involves a 'tendency to simply invoke theoretical precepts as axioms and then apply them to practice in an illustrative manner' (Kester 2011: 58). Similarly, Rule and Levine (2012) are critical of the reappropriation by artists of what they perceive as the abstruse language of the translated French texts. To examine this phenomenon further, they analysed a corpus of press announcements in the online arts magazine *e-flux* to establish the grammatical and lexical character of this type of theoretically inspired art writing. They found that it involves the overuse or misuse of a number of linguistic forms, including nominalisation, spatial and field metaphors, prefixes, adverbial phrases, lists, dependent clauses and definite articles, as well as lexical items such as *space, proposition, tension, interrogates, encodes, transforms, visuality* or *globality*. Their study has been highly influential and is frequently mentioned in the many websites produced to provide advice on the writing of the artists' statement.

While the studies mentioned above have either directly or indirectly considered the relationship between language and visual arts practice, including the observation of how certain emergent discourses affect change in the practices of artists, there has been no study to date that has specifically explored this relationship through an in-depth diachronic, corpus-based investigation of changing trends in the language used by artists to describe their own creative practices. Furthermore, no study has examined whether there is an alignment between shifts over time in the way that artists have described their artistic practices and changes that have taken place in everyday language use. Before moving on to the analysis of diachronic trends in the ALC, the following section describes and justifies the methods, analytical procedures and statistical measures used throughout this Element.

2 Methods

2.1 Corpus Analysis and the Investigation of Artists' Language

In order to investigate shifts in the way that artists in English-speaking contexts have used language to conceptualise their art practice from 1950 to 2019, and establish whether these shifts align with changes in the wider English lexicon, a 235,000-word diachronic corpus consisting of a collection of artists' interviews and statements about their work was created. Referred to as the Artists' Language Corpus (ALC), the corpus was first examined using the corpus analytical resources of Modern Diachronic Corpus Assisted Discourse Studies (MD-CADS) (Partington et al., 2008; Partington, 2010; Baker, 2011; Baker et al., 2013). The results of these analyses were then compared with the Corpus of Historical American English (Davis, 2010).

Corpus analysis, which can assist in the identification of language usage and patterns in representative collections of authentic texts (Baker, 2006), provides a useful analytical resource for examining the ALC to establish how artists use language to conceptualise their creative practices. Furthermore, corpus software enables texts to be tagged and analysed according to the particular periods when they were produced (Partington, 2010; Baker et al., 2013; Brezina, 2018; Marchi, 2018), providing, in this case, opportunities for identifying how visual arts practices are differently conceptualised over time. The following sections describe the methodology used for this study, including details of the ALC, the Sketch Engine corpus software and the specific corpus analytical techniques used for this Element.

2.2 Description of the Artists' Language Corpus

Taking into account the difficulties of obtaining an adequately representative and non-biased sample of specific language use from a larger target population to create a specialised language corpus (McEnery et al., 2006; Clear, 2011), this section provides a detailed description of the ALC. The texts collected for the ALC consist of artists' interviews and statements from 1950–2019. The start date of 1950 was chosen for the corpus as this was the earliest decade when it was possible to easily find a suitable number of accessibly available texts involving artists discussing or writing specifically about their work. Indeed, it was not until the 1950s, when a number of art magazines emerged, such as *Tiger's Eye* and *Possibilities*, that artists regularly began to present first-person accounts of their practices to the public (Liese, 2013). For the artists' interviews, all interview questions were omitted, so that only the artists' responses were included in the corpus data. Furthermore, where possible, only those parts of the interview that focussed on artists' discussions of their practice were included and parts such as the discussion of personal history were omitted. Overall, the corpus includes 337 unique texts.

The online corpus tool Sketch Engine (Kilgarriff, Baisa, Bušta et al., 2014), which was used for the analysis, indicates that the corpus contains 235,392 tokens. Although this might be considered within the upper limits of a small corpus, which according to Aston (1997) typically contains between 20,000 and 250,000 words, in a contemporary corpus-analytical context, where very large corpora are the norm, this would be considered fairly small. As mentioned, the overall size of the ALC was largely governed by the number of suitable and reliable texts that could be located for the earlier decades and the decision that the separate divisions of the corpus should contain a similar number of words. While difficulties sourcing data are often suggested as constituting a valid rationale for the size of a corpus (Bowker and Pearson, 2002; Brezina, 2018), small corpora are also widely viewed as suitable for the analysis of specialised language. Bowker and Pearson (2002), for example, have stated that 'anywhere from a few thousand to a few hundred words have proved useful for LSP studies' (p. 54) and Walsh (2013), who identifies a tendency towards the use of smaller context-specific corpora for the analysis of specific language forms, has discussed the practicability of conducting a small-scale research project on a specific context using a corpus of around 100,000 words. Similarly, Vaughan and Clancy (2013) suggest that many small corpora within the 20,000-to -50,000-word range have proved useful for analysing the pragmatic features of a specialised language. Small context-specific corpora are also seen as offering advantages over larger corpora because the user is more likely to be acquainted with both the original texts and the wider context from which the texts originate. This familiarity also provides greater opportunities for the interrogation and interpretation of findings (Aston, 1997; Koester, 2010), and is viewed as particularly essential for the analysis of diachronic corpora (Rissanen, 2018). Table 1 provides details of the composition of the ALC.

As can be seen in Table 1, the ALC has been divided into time intervals representing each of the calendar decades between 1950 and 2019. This divides the ALC into seven manageable units for the diachronic comparison (Baker et al. 2013). This division of the corpus into calendar decades also aligns with the majority of published texts that, when discussing historical shifts in the art world, typically make a distinction between the art of different decades (e.g., the art of the 1960s). Where texts had more than 1,000 words, only the first 1,000 words were included, or alternatively, if the initial stages of the text focussed on the discussion of the artists' personal history, then given the particular focus of the study, the first 1,000 words involving the explicit discussion of the artists'

Table 1 Word composition of the ALC

Time interval	Tokens	Types	TTR	%	Texts	Average words per text
1950–1959	23,612	3,808	62.0%	10	43	549
1960–1969	35,279	4,217	82.6%	15	50	706
1970–1979	35,297	4,341	81.3%	15	50	706
1980–1989	35,303	4,537	77.8%	15	50	706
1990–1999	35,296	4,771	74.0%	15	43	821
2000–2009	35,292	5,279	66.9%	15	50	706
2010–2019	35,313	5,089	69.4%	15	51	692
Total corpus	235,392	32,042	73.4%	100	337	698

creative practices were selected. The selection of 1,000 words from each text enabled the creation of a reasonably sized corpus, without compromising the analysis by including longer texts from individual artists. As McEnery et al. (2006) point out, a corpus that includes text segments of a constant size is likely to be more balanced than a corpus of full texts. It will also avoid the appearance of individual stylistic peculiarities as generalities.

With the exception of the 1950s, each time interval represents 15 per cent of the ALC and contains approximately 35,300 words. The aim was to include similar word frequencies for each decade, allowing raw frequencies, rather than normalised frequencies, to be compared in the first analytical stage of this study (Section 3). Due to the difficulty of easily locating reliable interview texts and artists' statements for the 1950s, this time interval only represents 10 per cent of the corpus, and 23,612 words. For the same reason, it contains a higher percentage of artists' statements. Table 2 identifies the different texts that comprise the corpus. The average number of words for the texts in the 1990s was higher than in the other decades of the ALC and hence a comparatively lower number of texts was included in this decade.

The texts in the corpus were located from online interviews, art magazines, books, artists' webpages, online repositories, published journals, exhibition catalogues and videos of artists' interviews. All texts selected for the ALC were required to be those of practising visual artists, for example, sculptors, painters, installation artists or photographers. Texts representing commercial photography practices, musicians or student artists were not included in the corpus. Texts were required to be produced originally in English and hence the majority of the texts represented artists from English-speaking contexts. Texts representing artists whose first language was not English were not excluded, however, as long as there was no indication the text had been translated from another language.

Table 2 Text composition of the ALC

Time interval	Interviews	Artists' statements	Total
1950–1959	10	33	43
1960–1969	34	16	50
1970–1979	37	13	50
1980–1989	33	17	50
1990–1999	32	11	43
2000–2009	32	18	50
2010–2019	34	17	51

The artists represented in each decade of the ALC include emerging artists, artists in the prime of their careers, as well as artists in the later stages of their careers. It might be argued that this last group is more likely to foreground discourses from prior decades in their interviews, thus potentially preventing the identification of certain shifting diachronic language trends in the corpus. However, the language used by more established artists to discuss their creative practices is also influenced by discursive shifts in the contemporary artworld and beyond, as are the foci of the questions asked by interviewers that serve as catalysts for the interview data collected for the ALC. As a result, while the texts in each decade all represent different artists, thirty-six artists feature across more than one decade. Furthermore, the dominant art discourses of prior decades are still relevant if they continue to occur in subsequent decades, even though they might be less pronounced in the interview data. Indeed, older discourses can continue to impact on current and future conceptualisations of art practice.

In order to provide a cursory indication of the wider consistency of the ALC, Table 3 lists the fifteen most frequent nouns for each decade of the corpus. The search that produced the results in the table focussed on lemmas, rather than individual word forms. A lemma refers to all of the inflections of a base word (Brezina, 2018). For example, in Table 3 the noun *painting* refers

Table 3 Most frequent fifteen nouns (lemmas) for each decade of the ALC

1950s	art, painting, artist, thing, work, form, time, way, picture, sculpture, painter, life, world, space, idea
1960s	art, painting, thing, work, way, time, something, colour, people, artist idea, kind, form, space, piece
1970s	work, painting, thing, art, way, time, something, people, kind, piece, idea, sculpture, artist, image, space
1980s	thing, work, art, painting, way, piece, people, time, kind, image, something, space, colour, artist, lot
1990s	work, painting, people, thing, way, time, something, art, idea, image, woman, kind, object, picture, artist
2000s	work, painting, art, way, people, time, thing, artist, world, kind, piece, image, something, idea, process
2010s	work, art, thing, way, painting, time, artist, people, something, image, idea, lot, body, year, world
All decades	work, art, painting, thing, way, time, people, something, artist, idea, kind, image, piece, space, colour

to both the singular noun *painting* as well as the plural noun *paintings* and therefore both inflections will be included in the frequency count. Similarly, the lemma of the verb *paint* would include the verb inflections *paints*, *painted* and *painting*. Throughout this Element, and unless stated, all frequency counts are those of lemmas representing a particular part of speech category. There are, however, debates as to whether inflections of a lemma should be conflated in corpus search results (Hoey, 2005). This is because a difference in the meaning of an inflectional form of a lemma might be overlooked or because each individual word tends to have its own unique collocational behaviour. However, given that this study has a discourse, rather than syntactical, focus, the search for lemmas rather than unique word types, was found to be the most useful. Hoey (2005) has also found working with lemmas, rather than individual words, beneficial.

Table 3 shows that the seven nouns *art*, *painting*, *artist*, *work*, *time*, *thing* and *way* all appear in the fifteen most frequent nouns of each decade, while the nouns *people*, *idea*, *image*, *kind*, *space* and *something* appear in at least four of the seven lists. Only six nouns – *painter*, *life*, *woman*, *object*, *process*, *body* and *year* – occur once in the table, and of these, *life*, *object*, *process* and *year* all appear in the 100 most frequent nouns for each decade of the ALC. The nouns *woman* and *body* (a frequent focus of feminist art) do not regularly occur in the most frequent words of a decade until the 1990s, most likely because female artists were both underrepresented and underacknowledged in the earlier parts of the twentieth century (Nochlin, 1971). Furthermore, the noun *painter* substantially drops from the 100 most frequent words of each decade from the 1990s onwards, which is most likely representative of the increasing decline in the identity of the painter in the arts throughout the twentieth century. The noun *painting*, however, maintains its place in the five most frequent words for each of the seven decades in the ALC. Overall, Table 3 shows that as well as containing similar high frequency nouns associated with art practice, each decade of the ALC contains similar high frequency shell or low content nouns (Schmid, 2000), such as *thing*, *way* and *kind*. These shell or low content nouns also typically appear in lists of the most frequent nouns of many reference corpora.

2.3 Methods

Methodologically, the study draws on the corpus analytical approaches often associated with Modern Diachronic Corpus Assisted Discourse Studies (Partington & Drugid, 2008; Partington, 2010). Modern Diachronic Corpus Assisted Discourse Studies, or MD-CADS, is a term increasingly used to refer to a diverse range of studies that employ corpus analytical resources to examine the impact of changes or stability in language use over time, with a particular focus on the construction of how political or sociocultural issues and practices are differently represented at different times (Partington et al. 2013; Marchi, 2018). As seen in the description of the ALC, MD-CADS uses diachronic or historical corpora; that is, corpora that sample 'different stages of language or discourse development across time' (Brezina, 2018: 221), and whose texts have been tagged according to the date of their production in order to facilitate the identification of temporal shifts (or stability) in language use. The specific corpus method used to establish trends in the artists' use of language over time involves trend mapping, although this is supported by the more traditional corpus tools used to carry out a discourse analysis of large collections of texts, such frequency, collocation and concordance analysis (Baker, 2006).

2.3.1 Trend Mapping

Stanyer and Mihelj (2016) suggest that the most common approach employed in MD-CADS is trend mapping. They describe trend mapping as focussing on 'examining the development of a chosen phenomenon over time, focusing on trends (decline, growth, fluctuations)' (p. 269) and state that trend mapping treats time as a continuum, as opposed to discrete temporal units. The approach to trend mapping in this study was twofold. First, it involved identifying lemmas that exhibited statistically significant increasing or decreasing frequency trends over the seven decades of the ALC. This employed the Sketch Engine trends tool, which identifies trends in a corpus using the Theil-Sen estimator and the Mann-Kendall tests. The non-parametric Theil-Sen estimator provides a linear approximation of the slope of the frequencies of a lemma, etc. over time by calculating the medium slope between all individual pairs of frequency points (in this case, the frequencies of a lemma for each decade). In Sketch Engine, the Theil-Sen slope is represented both as an arrow and as a numerical value that identifies the direction and magnitude of the trend. The arrow has three levels for each polarity. A flat arrow represents a trend between 0 and 0.1 (or –0.1), the lower level arrow represents a trend that is between 0.1 (or –0.1) and 1 (or –1) inclusive, while the higher level arrow represents a trend that is greater than 1 (or –1). According to Herman and Kovář (2013) the Theil-Sen estimator provides superior estimates of the slope of a trend when compared to ordinary regression models, especially on inferior data sets. The software also employs the Mann-Kendall test to identify the significance level of the trend statistic by

Figure 1 Sketch Engine trend information for the verb *explore*

providing a p-value.[2] Figure 1 provides an example of Sketch Engine's trend information for the verb *explore* in the ALC.

In Figure 1 the arrow provides a visual indication of the strength and direction of the trend, while the following value (1.15) represents this numerically. Next is the overall frequency of the verb *explore* in the corpus (52), after which there is an indication of the p-value (0.0068). The smaller the p-value, the less likely that the statistical results could have occurred by chance. In general, a p-value of less than 0.05 is used to indicate statistical significance. Finally, a sparkline is provided as a visual summary of the distribution of the frequencies over time. In corpus analysis, different search criteria are often selected so as to interrogate the corpus data in different ways. Hence, Sketch Engine allows decisions to be made regarding the preferred minimum frequency and maximum p-value. There is also the option of determining how the results of a trend analysis are sorted. The criteria used for each of the trend analyses will be identified in Section 3.

Second, in order to consider in more detail those lemmas indicating an increasing or decreasing trend, figures were created to enable a visual representation of the frequencies of lemmas over the seven decades of the ALC. An example can be seen in Figure 2, which displays a line graph indicating the frequency over time of the verb *explore*. While there are a few troughs and peaks, the figure shows (with the aid of a dotted exponential trendline) that overall, the use of the verb *explore* has steadily increased over time in the corpus. It should be noted that the solid points in the figure represent the frequency of *explore* for the whole decade identified in the x-axis, while the line between the points is simply used to provide an indication of the verb's trend over time.

When the figures are only used to identify the frequencies over time of lemmas in the ALC alone, raw frequency data is used, as seen in Figure 2. This is, first, because the frequencies in the ALC are often small and normalising these to the commonly used 'words per million' (a feature also provided by Sketch Engine) may have the effect of misrepresenting the actual size of frequency counts. Second, and as mentioned above, with the exception of the 1950s, the other decades of the corpus contain approximately 35,300 words,

---

[2] A more in-depth explanation and justification of the statistical methods used to establish the trend information in Sketch Engine can be found in Herman and Kovář (2013).

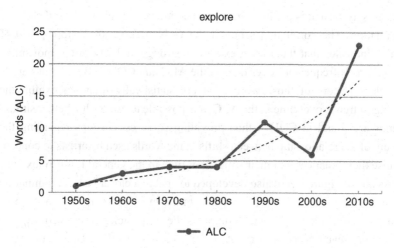

Figure 2 Frequency of the verb *explore* over time in the ALC with trendline

enabling raw frequency counts to be used. Given that the 1950s is the only period with a lower overall word count, it was decided not to normalise its frequency counts.

2.3.2 Comparison of Trends with COHA

As mentioned in Section 1, the second stage of this Element examines whether the diachronic shifts found in artists' use of language in the ALC align with those found in the wider English lexicon. The Corpus of Historical American English (COHA) was used for this comparison because it is the most extensive and generically balanced diachronic corpus of the English language, containing more than 475 million words from the 1820s to the 2010s (Davis, 2010). It is also segmented by decade and has an easily accessible and comprehensive online interface. As such, it provides a particularly suitable corpus for making comparisons with the findings from the ALC.

The process for the comparison involved, first, the use of a correlation analysis to determine the degree to which the change over time in the two corpora converges or diverges.

This was calculated using the CORREL function in Excel, which uses the Pearson Product-Movement Correlation Coefficient to determine the relationship between two sets of values. The two sets of values used in this case are the frequencies per million of the lemma for each of the seven decades for the two corpora. The CORREL function provides a correlation score between 1 and -1. The closer the correlation score is to 1, the more closely related is the movement over time of the lemma in the two corpora, while the closer the score is to -1, the less closely related is the movement of the lemma over time. A 0 indicates no correlation. The correlation score of the verb *explore*, for example, is 0.91 which indicates that there is an extremely strong similarity in the movement of the verb's frequencies over time in the ALC and COHA. By examining the correlation score of those words that are statistically found to exhibit the strongest trends over time in the ALC, it is possible to establish whether similar trends are found in COHA, thus providing some conclusions regarding the nature of the relationship between shifts in the words used by artists to conceptualise their practices and their shifts over time in the general English lexicon.

As above, figures were also developed to enable a closer visual examination of the relationship over time of specific lemmas in the two corpora. An example can be seen in Figure 3, which compares the frequencies of the verb *explore* across the seven decades of the ALC with those of COHA. Due to the often vastly different total word sizes of the two sets of corpora, the frequencies in these figures have been normalised to 'frequency per million words', a statistical measurement provided by both Sketch Engine and COHA. However, even with normalisation, there are still considerable differences between the frequencies being compared, typically because the words analysed are, in most cases, particularly salient for the ALC. For example, and as can be viewed in the 2010 period of Figure 2, *explore* has a normalised frequency of 651 words per million in the ALC and a normalised frequency of 55 words per million in COHA. As a result of this considerable difference, the figure also contains different scales for the y-axis (frequencies) but keeps the x-axis (decades) aligned. The result enables a more accessible visual comparison of

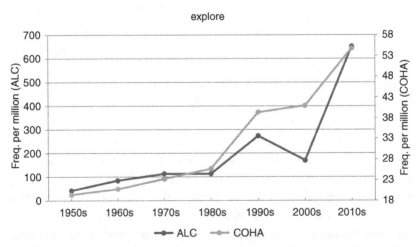

Figure 3 Frequency comparison of the verb *explore* in the ALC and COHA

shifts in the frequency data over time. In Figure 3, for example, it can be seen that the increase over time in the normalised frequencies of *explore* in the ALC align relatively closely with those in COHA. The only exception is in the 2000s where a noticeable dip is evident in the ALC.

2.3.3 Concordance Analysis

In order to find out more about the discourses constitutive of visual arts practice, how these are manifested in the language of the artists represented in the ALC and how they change over time, it is necessary to move beyond statistical methods and engage in a close qualitative examination of relevant language data in the corpus (Baker, 2006: Egbert, Larsson and Biber, 2020). A common way that this qualitative dimension is brought to quantitative findings in corpus research is through the examination of concordance lines. Concordance lines list all the instances of a particular search term from a corpus in the context of its surrounding text. Table 4 provides a list of concordance lines containing the verb *explore* from the 2010 decade of the corpus. Bold type is used in the concordance tables to identify aspects of concordance lines that are of specific interest and therefore usually discussed in the subsequent analysis.

The concordance lines in Table 4 can, first, provide information about the phenomena that artists typically 'explore'. It is evident from the table that these phenomena are often abstract nouns (e.g., *concept, essence, idea(s), aspects, potential*), many of which are directly complemented by another noun, often in the form of a prepositional phrase (e.g. *the essence of an image, ideas of identity, the potential of moments*). Moreover, when the artists' creative explorations do not involve an abstract concern, they often focus on aesthetic forms of their practice (*the circular form, colours, patterns*). A further concordance search of the ALC finds that of the fifty-two occurrences of *explore* in the corpus, forty-three collocate with abstract nouns. Of these, twenty-six are either directly or indirectly complemented by another noun, while seventeen involve the form of a prepositional phrase. The other nine instances of *explore* in the ALC involve a focus on aesthetic forms. Additionally, in lines 1, 2 and 5 artists conceptualise the artwork as the agent of the exploration, while in lines 4 and 7 they conceptualise themselves as the agent of the exploration. Line 6, however, includes their viewers in the explorative process.

Throughout this Element, the concordance tables provided usually contain lines selected from a larger set of concordance lines with the same node lemma in order to represent the key observations of the concordance analyses. There will be other concordance lines containing the node lemma that were not

Table 4 Concordance lines with the verb *explore* from the 2010 decade of the ALC

1	I'm currently working on a series of linocuts	exploring	the concept of 'hauntings'. I'm interested in how we
2	we find ourselves. Like the haiku, **my work**	explores	**the essence of an image**, memory, or moment in time.
3	in multiples. It is a way to learn about each form and	explore	an **idea**. The repetition becomes increasingly meditative.
4	a circle has closed. This is why I continually	explore	the **circular form** in the Portals series.
5	the versatility of the medium. **My painting**	explores	**colours and patterns** reflected in the exposed surface
6	the work, frequently challenging **the viewers to**	explore	with me **ideas of identity**, ancestry
7	and on my creativity. It's allowed **me** to	explore	**aspects of art history** that I probably wouldn't have been
8	an image I see or even have in my mind, but to	explore	**the potential of moments** I can only begin to imagine.

selected for the concordance table, but still support similar observations and there will also be lines from the same set that do not support the findings discussed. To ensure the representative of the concordance lines selected from the ALC, each line in each of the concordance tables in this Element has also been selected from a different text in the ALC. Furthermore, and as seen in Table 4, notable aspects of the selected concordance lines discussed in the analysis will be highlighted in bold in the concordance tables.

2.3.4 Collocation Analysis

Collocation analysis can also prove useful for diachronic corpus-assisted discourse analyses. Collocates are words that frequently co-occur, either immediately next to, or within a few words of, one another. Given that words are inclined to acquire meaning through their relationships with other words in a text, a collocation analysis is useful for revealing the types of connotation that a particular word embodies within a specific context (Hoey 2005; Baker 2006). With a diachronic corpus, a collocation analysis can also be used to establish how certain collations and their occurrences change over time. As an example, Baker et al. (2013) carried out a collocation analysis of the top ten immediate right-hand collocates of *Islamic* in a corpus of British newspapers for each year from 1998 to 2009. Some of the notable shifts over time included references to *Islamic fundamentalism*, which ceased to appear in the top ten collocates after 2004, and references to *Islamic terrorism*, which only began to appear in the top ten collocates after 2001.

Focussing again on exploration discourses, Table 5 lists the ten most frequent noun collocates of the verb *explore* for each decade from 1900 until 2000 in the Corpus of Historical American English (COHA). This was calculated using the COHA interface. The search included noun collocates located within a four-word span to the right of *explore*, so as to capture those nouns that may have been immediately preceded by other word forms, for example *explore this new land*. Furthermore, a mutual information (MI) score of 3 was selected as this is generally viewed as evidence that two items are collocates (Hunston, 2002).[3] It also typically favours low-frequency collocates that have an exclusive relationship. Only those collocates with more than one occurrence were included in the list. The aim of this collocation analysis is to identify whether the historical use of the verb *explore* in the wider English lexicon might provide any further insights into the emergent conceptualisation of art practice as an exploration in the early to mid-twentieth century.

---

[3] Mutual information is a statistic that indicates collocational strength. The higher the MI score, the less likely the two items will have co-occurred by chance (McEnery et al., 2006).

Table 5 Most frequent noun collocates of the verb *explore* from 1900 until 2000
in COHA (0/+4, MI ≥ 0)

Decade	Noun collocates
1900s	land, stream, country, mystery, river, town, room
1910s	region, cave, ground, headwater, neighbourhood, canyon, interior, mystery, detail, island
1920s	country, mountain, island, depth, sea, part, recess, tomb, route, region
1930s	possibility, region, situation, world, wanderings, depth, distance, river, country
1940s	possibility, path, mystery, field, problem, mind, city
1950s	possibility, territory, idea, avenue, relationship, truth, subject, river, area, ore
1960s	possibility, space, avenue, planet, moon, area, idea, problem, implication, material
1970s	world, possibility, problem, planet, oil, area, countryside, implication, island, opportunity, relationship
1980s	possibility, issue, area, system, oil, space, phenomenon, depth, avenue, connection
1990s	world, possibility, issue, space, idea, depth, potential, region, relationship, theme
2000s	option, possibility, career, effect, relationship, river, experience, surroundings, nature, sexuality
2010s	world, cover, possibility, relationship, option, aspect, environment, factor, effect, interaction

The table shows that from 1900–20 *explore* is predominantly used in a literal sense to refer to the exploration of geographic phenomena (*land*, *streams*, *rivers*, *mountains*). However, by the 1930s, *explore* begins to be more frequently associated with abstract phenomena, such as *possibility* and *situation*. This metaphoric use of *explore* steadily increases, so that by the 2010s, *explore* frequently collocates with a distinct range of abstract nouns including *option*, *effect*, *experience*, *relationship*, *issue*, *idea* and *potential*, among others. Table 5 suggests that the emergence of artists' metaphorical use of the verb *explore* corresponds with a similar increase in the metaphorical use of *explore* in the wider English lexicon and therefore provides some preliminary support for the view of a relationship between wider English usage and the language choices used by artists (at least in English-speaking contexts) to conceptualise their creative practices. In diachronic corpus linguistics, this noticeable shift in the use of *explore* that appears to have taken place in the 1930s has been referred to as a 'turning point' (Stanyer and Mihelj, 2016). A turning point refers to a particular moment in time when potentially lasting change can be observed. The relationship between the wider English lexicon and the findings from the analysis of the ALC will be presented in Section 4.

3 Changing Trends in Artists' Conceptualisation of their Creative Practices

3.1 Trend Analysis

The first stage of the examination into the changes that have taken place in artists' use of language to conceptualise their practice since the 1950s involved a trend analysis using the Sketch Engine Trends function (Kilgarriff et al., 2015). The aim of this first trend analysis was to identify the high frequency lemmas in the ALC that exhibited the strongest decreases and increases across the seven decades of the corpus. To achieve this, only those lemmas that occurred a minimum of fifty times in the corpus were included. This decision was influenced by Baker (2011), who stipulated that a word would need to occur at least 1,000 times to be of value for his study of diachronic variation involving a corpus of approximately 4 million words, and Lazzeretti (2016), who required a word to occur 100 times in her similar study of a diachronic corpus containing 378,315 words. In the ALC corpus, 479 unique words (or 480 lemmas) met the cut-off requirement of fifty occurrences, a number comparable, given the relative size of the ALC, to the cut-off requirements of both Baker and Lazzeretti. It was also decided to only include those lemmas that had a minimum Sketch Engine trend value higher than 1 for increasing trends, and less than -1 for decreasing trends.[4] This was to ensure that only those high-frequency lemmas exhibiting a relatively strong slope over time were included in this first trend analysis. Finally, a minimum p-value of 0.05 was used. This was to ensure that the results of the first trend analysis exhibited statistical significance (McEnery et al., 2006; Brezina, 2018). As seen in Table 6, the trend search using these criteria produced twenty-eight results.

As a way to help structure the analysis of these increasing and decreasing trends, the lemmas in Table 6 were arranged into eight semantically related groups. The eight groups are:

1 Media and modes (*performance, technology, medium, painter, canvas*). Of these, the nouns *performance, technology* and *medium* exhibit an increasing trend, while the nouns *painter* and *canvas* exhibit a decreasing trend. The

---

[4] These higher level trends are represented in Sketch Engine by an arrow with an increased slope.

Table 6 High frequency trending lemmas in the ALC (freq. $\geq$ 50, p < 0.05)

Rank	Lemma	POS	Trend	Direction	Freq.	P-value
1	performance	noun	2.48	↑	64	0.016
2	project	noun	2.48	↑	89	0.035
3	technology	noun	1.80	↑	51	0.035
4	medium	noun	1.73	↑	94	0.016
5	exhibition	noun	1.60	↑	76	0.035
6	bit	noun	1.54	↑	81	0.016
7	painter	noun	−1.48	↓	137	0.016
8	allow	verb	1.43	↑	75	0.035
9	involve	verb	−1.43	↓	114	0.035
10	true	adjective	−1.43	↓	65	0.007
11	memory	noun	1.38	↑	61	0.035
12	nothing	noun	−1.28	↓	101	0.035
13	word	noun	−1.28	↓	162	0.035
14	statement	noun	−1.28	↓	50	0.035
15	also	adverb	1.23	↑	347	0.007
16	must	modal	−1.23	↓	136	0.016
17	create	verb	1.19	↑	188	0.016
18	canvas	noun	−1.19	↓	101	0.016
19	language	noun	1.15	↑	85	0.035
20	certainly	adverb	−1.15	↓	56	0.016
21	explore	verb	1.15	↑	52	0.007
22	actually	adverb	1.11	↑	121	0.007
23	no	-	−1.11	↓	550	0.007
24	order	noun	−1.11	↓	83	0.016
25	any	-	−1.07	↓	331	0.016
26	read	verb	1.07	↑	77	0.016
27	choose	verb	1.07	↑	64	0.035
28	only	adjective	−1.04	↓	76	0.016

Note: *no* and *any* involve multiple parts of speech and these are not recognised by Sketch Engine.

noun *medium* also includes the plurals *media* (freq. 41) and *mediums* (freq. 8).

2 Practice (*project, exhibition*). These nouns loosely relate to art as a professional practice.

3 Constitutive verbs (*allow, involve, create, explore*). These are verbs used by artists to conceptualise, and also to rationalise, their creative actions. Of these verbs, only *involve* exhibits a decreasing trend.

4 Absoluteness and high modality (*true, nothing, must, certainly, no, only, any*). These items, which all exhibit a decreasing trend, are typically used in the ALC to express absoluteness or high modality. They are often found in the early decades of the ALC in proclamatory statements about visual artists and art practice (e.g. *the true creative artist has a powerful urge*) or, in the case of *no*, to dismiss outright the comments of the interviewer.

5 Themes (*memory*). *Memory* is the only lemma in this group and it exhibits an increasing trend in the corpus. It is frequently used as a thematic catalyst for art practice.

6 Language (*word, statement, language, read*). In this group, *word* and *statement* exhibit a decreasing trend and *language* and *read* exhibit an increasing trend.

7 Artistic choice (*choose, order*). These forms are often employed in a similar way to those in group 3, but tend to emphasise the artistic actions discussed as either the personal choice of artists (e.g. *the love of light is my inspiration and informs all the subjects I choose*), or as explanations for the choices made (e.g. *in order to find out about the past, I have to dig into the past*). *Order*, which exhibits a decreasing trend in the corpus, is also used to refer to the ordering of materials or as a synonym of *control*. *Choose* exhibits an increasing trend in the ALC and *order* exhibits a decreasing trend. From a discourse perspective, these items are of only minor interest and will not be examined further.

8 Rhetorical forms (*actually, also, bit*). These words are commonly used in the ALC to signal emphasis, addition or quantity. They exhibit an increasing trend in the corpus and, interestingly, also show a substantial increase in usage over time in the reference corpus COHA. However, they are not of particular interest for this study and therefore will not be examined further.

Groups 1–6 are analysed in more detail in the sections that follow. In some instances, the search criteria discussed above are adjusted to widen the scope of the analysis. These adjustments are identified in the relevant sections.

3.2 Media and Modes

The three related lemmas in this group, *performance, technology* and *medium*, exhibit some of the strongest increasing trends in the ALC (Table 6). The implication here is that one of the most significant shifts in the corpus over time is the increasing conceptualisation of art practice as primarily an engagement with the medium of the work and that this engagement has increasingly involved emerging *technology* and the proliferation of art as *performance*. In contrast, the two other lemmas in this group, *painter* and *canvas*, exhibit the strongest and eighth strongest decreasing trends in the ALC respectively. It might therefore be reasoned that a consequence of new emerging media and modes of artistic practice is the decline of traditional artistic identities (i.e. the painter) and the media traditionally associated with the practices of these identities (i.e. canvas).

In order to consider these implications further, concordance lines from the ALC containing *medium* were examined. Table 7 provides seven concordance lines representative of the twenty-eight occurrences of *medium* in the 2010s, while Table 8 provides concordance lines containing all four occurrences of *medium* in the 1960s.

In lines 1 and 6, in Table 7, the artists' construction of their artistic medium as producing a particular type of emotional response (i.e. exciting, challenging, evocative) is implicated as a motivation for their artistic work. In lines 1 and 2, the construction of their medium as having a specific function (i.e. offering messages, providing endless possibilities for storytelling) appears to motivate the artists' work, while in lines 3 and 4, a particular characteristic of their medium (peculiar, versatile) is constructed as motivating their work. Concordance lines 2–7 also provide a representation of the range of media

Table 7 Selected concordance lines with the noun *medium* from the ALC (2010s)

1	find **excitement** and **challenges** in the potential of the	medium	and the **messages that it has to offer us** today.
2	aspect of my art. One of the **greatest things** about **mixed**	media	is this sense of **endless possibility**. Practically
3	From the beginning I worked with **video** and I thought of the	medium	in terms of **what is peculiar to it**, as compared
4	into previous layers and really exploit the **versatility** of the	medium	My **painting** explores colours and patterns
5	to be really expressive of the emergence of **electronic**	media	things like **computer chips** and **computer networks**.
6	using sound as the material. **Sound** is a very **evocative**	medium	because you're using a musical vocabulary or a
7	my work and my community involvement. My primary	mediums	are **performance art**, **poetry** and **dance**, but my work also

Table 8 Selected concordance lines with the noun *medium* from the ALC
(1960s)

		medium	
1	be basically a mind sort of thing. **I can express it in any**	medium	just as you use water in everything for cooking.
2	once removed you're not as involved in metier, wrist or	medium	as is often the case with **oil**. At its best, it fights
3	secret of our inner voice. **It should not matter in what**	medium	**we try to express this**. I think of the child and the
4	**critics** use when communicating with each other through the	medium	of **art magazines**. Mini-art is best because it reminds one

and modes employed by artists in the 2010s (i.e. *mixed, sound, performance, painting, poetry, dance*), including media representative of new technology (i.e. *video, electronic, computer chips, computer networks*). Together, these concordance lines suggest that not only has art practice engaged with a greater range of media since the 1950s, but that the affordances of new and different media have become one of the primary motivations for engaging in art practice. Indeed, in line 2, the constitutive role of media is referred to as one of its *greatest things*. In stark contrast to the conceptualisation of media as shaping the contemporary creative act, of the only four occurrences of *medium* in the 1960s (Table 8), two involve artists explicitly identifying their ability to express an existing creative concept in any medium (lines 1 and 3). The two other concordance lines refer to the medium of oil paint (line 2), and the magazines in which critics publish their reviews (line 4).

As indicated earlier, a consequence of the emergence of media as constitutive of creative practice is that, over time, artists in the ALC have tended to be less concerned with the use of traditional artistic identities, such as that of *painter*. Figure 4 provides a visual representation of the significant decrease over time in the occurrence of *painter* in the ALC and shows how this contrasts with an increase in the use of *medium*. Interestingly, a wider examination of the ALC indicates that, unlike the earlier prevalence of the identity *painter*, those artists whose work is motivated by less traditional forms of artistic media tend not to construct their artistic identities as being aligned with the media they employ. Hence the identities *graffiti artist* and *sound artist*, for example, occur only once each in the ALC, while *performance artist, installation artist* and *video artist*, perhaps surprisingly, do not occur at all.

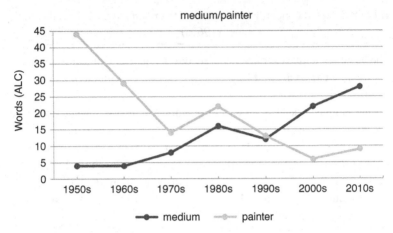

Figure 4 Frequency comparison of the nouns *medium* and *painter* in the ALC

Given the considerable frequency of *painter* in first two decades of the ALC, it is of interest to examine its use during these decades. Table 9 provides five concordance lines selected from the 1950s and 1960s. Overall, the lines in Table 9 show an explicit concern with constructing the wider identity of the painter and the practices with which they are associated. In line 1, for example, painters are viewed as not able to verbally articulate their visual practices and in line 2, they are constituted as capable of engaging in any painterly style. Similarly, in line 3, painters are constructed as requiring ethical values, while in lines 4 and 5, they are constructed as lacking concern with pictorial backgrounds, yet, as with sculptors, interested in space. It is of note that with the exception of line 1, which uses *should* to express strong obligation, the absence of modality conveys these propositions as objective and impersonal. Furthermore, only one concordance line (line 2) contains a pronominal reference to the artist who produced the text. As indicated in Section 2.3.3, each concordance line in Table 9 is selected from a different text in the ALC.

Conversely, the five selected concordance lines with *painter* representative of the 2010 decade of the ALC in Table 10, tend to indicate the speaker's more subjective personal concern with their own identity as a painter. This is evident in the prevalence of first-person pronouns in these concordance lines, the employment of personal narratives (lines 1 and 5), and self-reflection (lines 2 and 3).

The other noun in this semantic group, *performance*, exhibits the strongest increasing trend in the ALC, suggesting that the conceptualisation of art as performance is one of the more significant developments in the artworld since

Table 9 Selected concordance lines with the noun *painter* from the ALC (1950s and 1960s)

1	make it understood and least of all, the words of others. A	painter	**should never speak because words are not the means at his command.** (1950s)
2	apathy and want to lie down and go to sleep. Some	painters	including **myself, do not care what chair they are sitting on.** (1950s)
3	of consciousness Without ethical **consciousness**, a	painter	is only a decorator. Without **ethical** consciousness, the (1950s)
4	The question of painting in background is degrading for a	painter	The thing you want to express is not in that background (1960s)
5	space is made of. Sculptors talk about space,	painters	talk about space. Every artist has some kind of a definition (1960s)

Table 10 Selected concordance lines with the noun *painter* from the ALC (2010s)

1	that **my** painting teacher told **me** (he was a show car	painter).	He said: 'Judy, there is no such thing as perfection.'
2	**I** receive from creating. **I** consider **myself** a regional	painter	and **my** work is grounded in the visually dramatic
3	portraits was the best way for **me** to improve as a	painter	and **I** wasn't sure that **I** would really be able to
4	else's interpretation of a person, an Indian mystic	painter	and **my** drawings from that are a translation process. **I**
5	**me** a long time to develop. **I** was largely following other	painter's	footsteps and **I** was unable to have much critical discourse

the 1950s. As indicated in Figure 5, *performance* occurs a single time in both the 1950 and 1960 decades of the ALC and in each of these instances, it is used to conceptualise the act of painting as a performance. It is not until the 1970s that *performance* first occurs in the ALC to explicitly refer to the type of performance commonly associated with art practice that typically involves the body as an art medium (Robertson and McDaniel, 2017). As indicated in Figure 5, this close

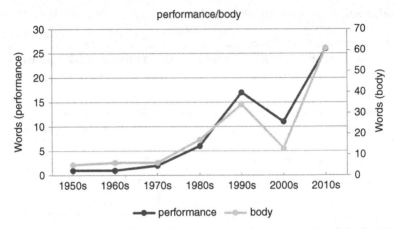

Figure 5 Frequency comparison of the nouns *performance* and *body* in the ALC

alignment between body and performance is also evident across the seven decades of the ALC.[5]

3.3 Practice

The lemmas *project* and *exhibition* exhibit the second and fifth strongest trends of those words having a frequency of fifty or greater in the ALC. *Project* rarely occurs in the corpus until the 1990s when an exponential increase takes place. Table 11 provides a representative selection of eight concordance lines from the 2000 and 2010 decades of the corpus containing the lemma *project*. Each line is selected from a different text in the ALC.

The concordance lines indicate the artists' use of the noun *project* as a synonym for their creative works. However, the use of *project* implies a more extensive, carefully planned and possibly collaborative undertaking and perhaps sits in contrast to the traditional perception of the solitary artist working on a single canvas in their studio. The concordance lines also indicate that the artist's project is constituted as a routine and regular activity (*previous, next one, many of my, every, latest*) with each project viewed as having a systematic connection to other projects. Associated with the use of *project* is the suggestion of a marketing discourse. This is evident, for example, in the reference to *sales, opportunities* and *press* in line 5 and the verb phrase *took on* in line 4, which constitutes the contemporary visual artist as a freelance professional whose activities are driven by the projects on offer at certain time periods. Interestingly, in lines 6 and 7, the project is constituted as

---

[5] In order to enable a more accessible visual comparison of frequency shifts of these two items over the seven decades of the ALC, each uses a different scale for the y-axis (see Section 2.3.2).

Table 11 Selected concordance lines with the noun *project* from the ALC (2000s and 2010s)

1	past. I always take something from a **previous**	project	and use it in the **next one**, creating a different (2010)
2	elusive, malleable shadow (body). In **many of my**	projects	over the past several years, including the (2010)
3	be destroyed. You know, it's almost as if **every**	project	or **every idea** becomes like a test. It becomes an (2010)
4	and culture as cues for living. I **took on** this	project	because I felt that it was the **right time** to apply (2010)
5	visibility, **sales, opportunities, press,** great	projects.	We live in a day an age where an artist **cannot just create** (2010)
6	the right mood. Sometimes **I have failed** and the	project	has been **very difficult**. I have found that the Cubes (2000)
7	as ever before, so in that sense the whole	project	was **a complete flop**. On the other hand, (2000)
8	redetermined narratives. The inspiration for my **latest**	project	came from a statistic released in the UK last year that (2000)

something that can fail. This suggests that art practice, when discursively conceptualised as a project, is understood as having planned outcomes.

Cicmil et al. (2016) suggest that a goal-oriented focus on already intended outcomes is an important characteristic of the 'project discourse', which they argue has increasingly pervaded contemporary society in recent decades. Nonetheless, a major influence on the increasing projectification of an artist's creative activities is emergence of postgraduate research in the visual arts in the 1970s (Elkins, 2009) and the consequent reshaping of the study of visual arts as 'practice-led research' that is undertaken through what are widely referred to as 'projects' or 'project-based investigations' (Allpress et al., 2012). In this context, the project is seen as replacing the established research model of the written thesis and hence has become the primarily vehicle for the creation of new knowledge in practice-based postgraduate study. It could be argued that the subsequent increase in the use of *project* to reference the creative work of artists and the word's particular relationship with the institutionalisation of art, impacts on the nature of contemporary art practice. An indication of this reshaping and one that aligns with the shifts in artistic identity mentioned in the previous section is evident in the following comment from an art educator (Schwarzenbach & Hackett, 2015):

> I guess I have some feelings about the art world that we are creating. I worry about something like painting fitting into this kind of format ... It's in the same way that Roberta Smith wrote that article about why no New York museums are showing painting because we are now trained to see art as being this kind of *project based* ... *institutional* thing, whether it is sculpture, installation, or video. And often painting doesn't fit into that format.
>
> (Schwarzenbach and Hackett, 2015: 120; emphasis added)

The comment also provides a link between the conceptualisation of art as a project and the conceptualisation of art as constituted by a variety of media, which was discussed in the previous section. In the ALC, the frequencies over time of the nouns *project* and *medium* share a very similar trajectory.

3.3.1 Art Practice and the Viewer

As indicated above, the increasing conceptualisation of artists' creative work as 'practice-led research undertaken through project-based investigations' (Allpress et al., 2012: 1) suggests a discursive connection between the two concepts 'project' and 'practice'. As seen in Figure 6, the frequencies over time of these two nouns share a relatively similar distribution in the ALC. Both rapidly increase from the 1980s, although *practice* exhibits a slight decline in the 2010s.

Indeed, as with the use of *project*, the widespread usage of *practice* to describe the creative work of artists is also comparatively recent. This is indicated in Figure 7, which shows the occurrence of the collocates *creative*

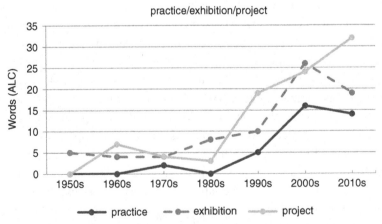

Figure 6 Frequencies of the nouns *practice*, *exhibition* and *project* over time in the ALC

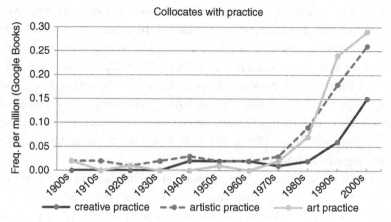

Figure 7 Frequencies of collocates with *practice* over time in the Google Books Corpus

practice, *art practice* and *artistic practice* in the 34-billion-word diachronic Google Book Corpus (British) (Davis, 2011). The Google Books Corpus (British) was used here due to its size, as these collocates were extremely rare in the one-billion-word COHA corpus. As can be seen in Figure 7, it was not until the 1980s that the wider conceptualisation of creativity as practice occurred in any substantial way. Furthermore, the occurrence of these three collocates with *practice* aligns with the overall occurrence in the ALC of *practice* (Figure 6), which does not occur in the corpus before the 1970s. Although the noun *practice* does not occur in Table 6 because it has a frequency less than fifty (freq. 37) in the ALC, it does exhibit a statistically significant increasing trend value of 2.71 (p < 0.05).

The increasing conceptualisation over time of art as 'practice' could also be argued as signalling a similar increase in a more audience-centred, interactive conceptualisation of art. Kemmis (2010), for example, draws attention to the extra-individual nature of practice to state that practices are not solely determined by the knowledge or agency of practitioners, but are predominantly constructed in interaction. By this he means that the clients of practitioners (in the case of the visual artists, 'viewers') are not merely acted on or influenced by practitioners, but are, in part, knowing subjects who participate in and are constitutive of practice. Focussing more specifically on the visual arts context, Miller (2017) states that defining art as practice constitutes it as 'an affective, productive phenomenon, decentring creativity to give the audience a full role in the doing of art' (p. 248) and similarly Wesner (2018) suggests that conceptualising art as practice fore-grounds the cooperative and social aspect of art.

In support of these perspectives, the lemma *viewer* (freq. 120) in the ALC corpus exhibits a considerable increase in frequency from the 1980s, a trajectory that aligns with the increase of the lemma *practice* in the corpus. It is of interest that in the early decades of the ALC, the few artists who mention their viewers construct them differently to the way they are constructed in the later decades of the ALC. This can be evidenced in a comparison of a representative sample of concordance linescontaining *viewer* from the 2010s (Table 12) with a representative sample of lines containing *viewer* from the 1960s (Table 13).

The role of the viewers as participants in the artists' practices is clearly evident in the concordance lines from the 2010s, where the viewers' subjective experiences (*introspection, intimacy, own memories, own identity*) are foregrounded as central to the aims of the work. Conversely, the selection of concordance lines containing the noun *viewer* from the 1960s, show that while the artists do acknowledge their audience as bringing their own interpretative capacity to the work, they perceive this as a potential conflict, or something that is regrettably beyond their control. Also, unlike the 2010s, artists from the 1960s appear to predetermine the nature of the viewers' interpretation of the work or desire that it occurs in a particular way (*a viewer would see, makes him realise, I would like the viewer to feel*). This shift in the function of *viewer* is resonant with Barthes (1967) notion of the 'death of the author' where he argues that the author is no longer seen as providing the definitive explanation of the text, which is instead generated through the reader's own individual interpretation. The synonym *audience* (freq. 48) is used less frequently by artists across the seven decades of the ALC. Nevertheless, *audience* also exhibits a steady increase over time throughout the corpus.

Table 12 Selected concordance lines with the noun *viewer* from the ALC (2010s)

1	allows an **introspection** and **intimacy** of the	viewers'	**experience**, perhaps sometimes missing in
2	the meditative quality of my work encourages	viewers	to draw upon their **own memories** and **experiences**
3	These 'words turned into pattern' allows the	viewer	to **engage more** with the work as they attempt to
4	sounds and scents. Often challenging the	viewer	to investigate their **own identity**, as well as
5	I like keeping the paintings **open** enough that a	viewer	can put some of **themselves** in it and **experience**

Table 13 Selected concordance lines with the noun *viewer* from the ALC
(1960s)

1	there was a **real conflict** there in terms of the	viewer.	It was hard to reconcile the wood as a colour
2	and you relate to it in a structural way. A	viewer	**would see** the colour, but then get into what's
3	a head it is only knowledge on the part of the	viewer	which **makes him realise** it is a head, but
4	I realised I would **not be able to control** the	viewer	to me, one of the important things about the
5	be convincing and satisfying. **I would like** the	viewer	**to feel that they** were worth looking at and would

3.3.2 Exhibition

Less can perhaps be said about the statistically significant increase over time of the lemma *exhibition* in the ALC corpus. The primary implication is that the exhibition as the vehicle through which the artist's work is introduced to their viewers is more of a concern to artists in the later decades of the corpus than it is to those in the earlier decades. Indeed, a statement from the 1950s of the ALC states that *Art existed before exhibitions . . . Art has nothing to do with exhibitions*. Furthermore, given that the frequency increase over time of *exhibition* in the ALC aligns closely with that of *project* (Figure 6), it might also be suggested that for artists in the later decades of the ALC, the conceptualisation of art as a project – which, as stated, implies a more extensive, carefully planned, and collaborative undertaking – considers the final exhibition of works as an integral component of the project. Moreover, as was indicated in the discussion of *project*, the exhibition also has an explicit connection with the viewer, overall suggesting a close lexical and conceptual synergy between *project, exhibition, practice* and *viewer*.

3.4 Constitutive Verbs

In Section 1.1, it was suggested that over time the language of certain discourses become entrenched in the lexicon of contemporary artists as constitutive of the natural and legitimate actions of art practice and that artists' deployment of this lexicon to facilitate their creative practices is evident in the explanations they provide about their works. It was also mentioned that central to these constitutive discourses are verb processes and their associated entailments or schemas. For example, at certain times artists have conceptualised their work as 'studying' or 'exploring' some phenomenon. 'Studying' is characteristically tied to the detailed scrutiny of an object, while 'exploring' is characteristically tied to a search for new and unfamiliar outcomes.

Six verb processes, *allow, involve, create, explore, read* and *choose*, appeared in the list of words in Table 6 that exhibited a statistically significant increase or decrease over time in the ALC corpus and also have a frequency of fifty or higher. Of these, it was determined that *allow, involve, create* and *explore* represent the types of constitutive verb that are discursively facilitative of visual arts practice, with all but *involve* exhibiting an increase over time in the ALC. Selected concordance lines from the corpus in Table 14 exemplify the facilitative role of these verbs. As usual, all concordance lines are selected from different texts in the ALC.

As seen in lines 1 and 2 – and in keeping with the characteristic schema of the verb *allow* – artists' creative acts are increasingly conceptualised as the permitting of an action that has previously been prevented or occluded. Lines 3 and 4 are representative of the conceptualisation of creative practice as the complete envelopment of the artist with some, often extraordinary, phenomenon or activity. However, given the significant decrease of *involve* over time in the

Table 14 Selected concordance lines with constitutive verbs from the ALC

1	Perhaps my work is just a magnifying lens that	allows	you to see the hidden details of reality. Every time I (2000)
2	Art is an experience designed to	allow	every individual to be and find themselves. (1980)
3	painting real places that I could see and I began to get	involved	with light sources, again. In Bradford one painted (1970)
4	one side to the other fifty-six that you become completely	involved	with both that inside space and the outside space or (1960)
5	diminishing what makes us different. My mission is to	create	worthwhile art experiences and continually expand my (2010)
6	the sound will hover in the rooms. We **wanted to**	create	an atmospheric intimacy; we don't want the bells to (2000)
7	program for adjudicated youth in DC. My work	explores	the unspoken and invisible social codes (2010)
8	and the work, frequently challenging the viewers to	explore	with me ideas of identity, ancestry and cultural (2010)

ALC, it would appear that this particular conceptualisation of creative practice is declining. Lines 5 and 6 represent the now pervasive conceptualisation of art practice as the bringing of some phenomenon or experience into existence and lines 7 and 8 provide examples of the previously discussed conceptualisation of creative practice as the artist's attempt to explore some phenomenon (Section 1.1).

Due to the particular importance of verbs for the conceptualisation of creative practice, it was decided useful to identify a greater number that exhibited statistically significant trends in the ALC. As a result, different criteria were employed for the trend analysis. The p-value of 0.05 or less to warrant statistical significance was maintained, but the minimum number of occurrences was reduced to eight.

The result of this change of criteria was the identification of 150 increasing and forty-two decreasing trends, forty-one of which were verbs. Following a qualitative examination of the concordance lines of these verbs, nineteen were designated as belonging to the group of constitutive verbs employed by artists to conceptualise their creative actions. These are listed in Table 15 and ordered according to the Theil-Sen trend statistic, which indicates the strength of their trend. The columns on the left side of the table show the frequency of the verb for each of the seven decades represented in the ALC.

At first glance, the findings in Table 15 might be viewed as somewhat insignificant because the frequencies of the verbs in the decades on the left-hand side of the table are quite small. However, besides the statistical support for their significance, the absence – or at least the relatively low frequencies – of the constituent verbs in the earlier decades of the ALC is revealing. As an example, the single occurrence of the lemma *examine* in approximately 129,500 words of artists' talk about their work, from the beginning of the 1950s until the end of the 1980s, is remarkable, especially given today's relatively frequent use of the verb in the same or similar context. Lazzeretti (2016), for example, in her corpus-assisted exploration of the language of museum communication, found that the word *examine* frequently occurred as a collocate of *exhibition* in the 2010s, particularly in the context of examining a certain artistic topic.

Table 16 provides a list of the phenomena found to co-occur as objects of the nineteen verb processes identified as trending upwards in the ALC. Overall, the table could be seen as listing many of the concepts that have salience in the contemporary art world. Words in italics occur more than once in the table and could be argued as having particular salience.

Of the total of forty-one verbs found in the second trend list generated by Sketch Engine (i.e. minimum freq. ≥ 8, $p < 0.05$), only four exhibited a significant decrease in frequency since the 1950s. They were *bother* (freq.

Table 15 Increasing constitutive verb trends in the ALC Corpus (freq. ≥ 8, $p < 0.05$)

Rank	Verb	Trend	Freq.	1950	1960	1970	1980	1990	2000	2010
1	examine	3.73	11	0	0	1	0	1	4	5
2	strive	3.49	8	0	0	0	0	1	3	4
3	capture	3.08	18	0	0	0	2	4	5	7
4	collect	2.90	12	0	0	0	2	4	1	5
5	inform	2.90	14	0	0	0	2	3	3	6
6	drive	2.48	17	0	1	1	2	3	4	6
7	connect	2.25	38	0	1	5	4	4	12	12
8	challenge	2.25	14	0	0	1	2	2	3	6
9	inhabits	1.88	9	0	0	1	2	2	2	2
10	influence	1.66	30	1	2	4	3	7	4	9
11	encourage	1.48	14	1	0	2	2	2	3	4
12	construct	1.48	29	0	2	5	2	9	5	6
13	allow	1.43	75	2	4	12	10	16	10	21
14	employ	1.43	10	0	1	0	1	2	5	1
15	combine	1.43	26	1	3	3	2	4	6	7
16	remind	1.38	15	0	1	1	3	1	7	2
17	create	1.19	188	8	13	10	25	29	31	72
18	explore	1.15	52	1	3	4	4	11	6	23
19	enjoy	1.07	35	3	3	3	5	6	5	10

Table 16 Objects of constitutive verbs exhibiting increasing trends

My work		
examines	topics, themes, states, relationships, situations, ideas	
strives for/to	simplicity, produce compelling work, balance formal and conceptual concerns, define questions, a physical dynamism	
captures	a likeness, my rage, their essence, a moment, an appearance, dreams, our attention, our belief, her body, a place, an image, movements, horse, world, expressions, exploding star or galaxy, experience	
collects	objects, stories, stuff, toys, memories, documents, files, inspirations	
is informed by	the subconscious, media, discourses, teaching, ideology, colour patterns, a perspective, culture, desire, the intangible, information, inspiration	
is driven by	questions, processes, ideas, investigations, desires, discovery	
connects	people, relationships, threads, things, ideas	
challenges	incongruities, the mainstream, paradigms, authority, the viewers, values, reality	
inhabits	space, the future	
is influenced by	ideas, topographies, scenes, impacts, backgrounds, circumstances, reflections, observations, perspectives	
encourages	a new aesthetic, awareness, people, viewers, dialogue, questions, the unexpected, the accidental	
constructs	worlds, images (x2), a space, a narrative (x2), a struggle, a piece, reality	
allows	various interpretations, new dimensions, seeing, engagement, introspection, experience, expression, self-discovery, progression of ideas, access, things to exist, imagination	

Table 16 (cont.)

employs	resources, techniques, *objects, systems*
combines	*processes,* different *aspects,* elements, *media, colours, forms*
reminds (me) of	fragility, the *beauty* of life, *strategies,* the physics of *colour,* wood block prints,
creates	*images, spaces, situations,* installations, music, environments, sound, *change,* language, *reality, systems, experiences,* senses, *objects,* sculptures, *form,* paintings, taxonomies, dissonance, diversions, friction, the sublime, *backdrops,* scandals, conundrums, confusion
explores	interests, notions, variables, the *world* (x2), complexities, *relations,* thresholds, *imagery, ideas,* feelings, *relationships, memories, media,* the *subconscious,* power, *questions,* qualities, *concepts, topics,* boundaries, *ideas, essences,* tributaries, making, *form, colours* (x2), *strategies, aspects, something,* figuration
enjoys	*observing, simplicity,* collaboration, representation, *form,* vocabulary, watching *change,* pleasure, subtleties, *working* big, *working* on paper, *physicality, colours,* composition *beauty*

12), *grasp* (freq. 10), *involve* (freq. 114) and *seem* (freq. 237). Of these, however, *involve* is the only verb regularly used by artists in the ALC to conceptualise art practice (see Table 14). Trends related to decreasing constitutive verbs will be discussed in the next section.

Overall, the sizeable difference between the number of increasing and decreasing verb trends potentially indicates that since the 1950s, artists have been deploying an ever increasing number of verbs to conceptualise their creative practices. To examine this proposition further, Figure 8 shows the total number of unique verb types for each decade of the ALC. It can be seen from the figure that from the 1950s until the 2000s there was a 39 per cent increase in the number of unique verb types used by artists in the ALC, with only a slight dip in the 2010s. This represents a considerable increase in number of unique verbs used over time and suggests that since the 1950s, artists have had a progressively growing range of verb processes from which to constitute their creative practices as part of their internalised lexicon.

3.4.1 Decreasing Constitutive Verbs in the ALC

As mentioned, the criteria for the trend analysis in Section 3.4 only returned four verbs that exhibited a decreasing trend and only one (*involve*) was identified as a verb used by artists to conceptualise their practices. As a result, the search criteria for the Sketch Engine Trend tool were adjusted again to include lemmas with a p-value of less than 0.1 (although keeping the previous minimum frequency of eight), in order to expand the number of constitutive verbs in the ALC that statistically indicate a continual decrease in frequency from the 1950s until the 2010s. The significance of the trend results produced are slightly compromised in that the likelihood of the results occurring by chance has increased from five per cent ($p < 0.05$) to ten per cent ($p < 0.1$).

The new criteria resulted in 371 trending lemmas. Of these, 267 exhibited increasing trends and 104 exhibited decreasing trends. Of the 104 lemmas exhibiting decreasing trends, fourteen are verbs and a closer examination of these verbs in their wider textual context indicated that only five appeared in the ALC as those used by artists to conceptualise their practices. These constitutive verbs are listed in Table 17, which also indicates the Theil-Sen trend statistic, the overall frequency of each verb in the ALC and the frequencies of the verbs in successive decades from the 1950s to the 2010s.

What is evident in Table 17 is that these constitutive verb process, with the exception of *involve*, all function semantically to describe the artist's work as an act *against* some undesirable phenomena. In contrast, and with the exception of *challenge*, the collective functions of the increasing constitutive verb processes

Table 17 Decreasing constitutive verb trends in the ALC Corpus (freq. ≥ 8, p < 0.1)

Rank	Verb	Trend	Freq.	1950	1960	1970	1980	1990	2000	2010
1	resolve	-3.49	10	4	1	4	0	1	0	0
2	free	-1.66	14	6	3	1	2	0	2	0
3	eliminate	-1.66	16	2	8	2	3	0	0	1
4	solve	-1.48	18	2	5	4	3	3	0	1
5	involve	-1.43	114	10	41	27	15	7	9	5

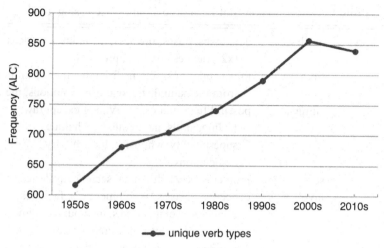

Figure 8 Number of unique verb types across the seven decades of the ALC

listed earlier in Table 15, act *with*, rather than against, existing phenomena, often in order to positively transform the phenomena in some way. In order to consider this observation further, Table 18 lists the objects that co-occur with these five constitutive verbs. As can be seen in the table, it appears that there is a tendency for art practice in the 1950s decade of the ALC to be conceptualised around the solution to a problem, paradox, crises or dilemma – or, similarly, the freedom from or elimination of some extant state, idea or phenomenon.

Of the nouns used to refer to an undesirable state, *problem* is the most frequent and occurs 150 times in the ALC. Figure 9 provides a graphic representation of the frequency of *problem* in the corpus, which reached a peak frequency of thirty-seven in the 1960s and a low frequency of eight in the 2000s. The decrease over time in the use of the noun *problem* from the 1950s to the 2010s provides support for the argument that visual arts practice around the mid-twentieth century was widely conceptualised as a need to (re)solve, eliminate or free oneself from a stated problem or undesirable state. Interestingly, there was no similar significant increase or decrease in the use of the number of semantically related nouns, *conflict* (freq. 17), *dilemma* (freq. 8), *paradox* (freq. 8) or *crisis* (freq. 4). The noun *secrets*, however, which was seen to collocate with *solve* in the ALC exhibited a decreasing trend statistic of -2.14 ($p < 0.05$).

3.5 Absoluteness and High Modality

In order to provide a slightly wider examination of those lemmas grouped as being semantically related to absoluteness or high modality, the search criteria

Table 18 Objects of constitutive verbs exhibiting decreasing trends

My work	resolves	paradoxes, crises, rawness, the unknown, ideas (x2), themes conflicts, problems
	frees	the unconscious, actions from the mind, painting from the naturalistic, one from emotions, me
	eliminates	possibilities, an idea, everything except raw feeling, skills, nature, text, technique, superficiality, whimsies, the arbitrary, associations
	solves	problems (x12), dilemma, secrets, mysteries
	involves	concerns, ideas (x4), volumes (x2), faculties, relations, seeing, effects, manipulation, images, participation, everyday crap, processes (x4), problem, seeing, mandalas, the surface, light sources, nuances, colour (x2), composition, making, shapes, identification, aspects

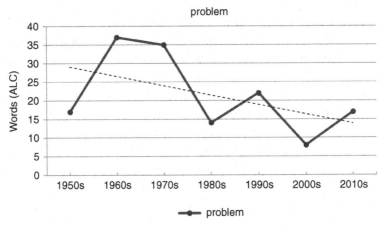

Figure 9 Frequency of *problem* over time in the ALC

from Section 3.4 were used again (freq. ≥8, $p < 0.05$). Of the forty-two lemmas found to have a decreasing trend using these criteria, thirteen have a semantic association with the expression of absoluteness or high modality. These thirteen lemmas, along with their part of speech, trend statistic, and frequency over time in the ALC, are listed in Table 19.

Table 19 Decreasing lemmas exhibiting a semantic association with absoluteness/high modality (freq. ≥ 8, $p < 0.05$)

Rank	Lemma	POS	Trend	Freq.	1950	1960	1970	1980	1990	2000	2010
1	unity	noun	-2.61	12	3	4	2	2	0	0	1
2	none	noun	-2.36	14	3	3	4	3	1	0	0
3	ought	modal	-1.66	10	5	2	1	1	1	0	0
4	pure	adjective	-1.48	38	8	10	4	6	4	3	3
5	true	adjective	-1.43	65	11	14	14	10	9	5	2
6	full	adjective	-1.33	36	7	7	6	6	6	3	1
7	nothing	noun	-1.28	101	18	13	23	17	14	10	6
8	must	modal	-1.23	136	32	23	27	17	18	14	5
9	certainly	adverb	-1.15	56	9	12	10	7	9	4	5
10	no	-	-1.11	550	152	107	75	81	58	40	37
11	order	noun	-1.11	83	15	13	18	12	10	7	8
12	any	-	-1.07	331	53	78	55	43	30	40	32
13	only	adjective	-1.04	76	10	17	15	14	8	8	4

Note: *no* and *any* represent multiple parts of speech and these are not recognised by Sketch Engine.

A closer investigation of concordance lines containing the words in Table 19 shows that some are often components of rhetorical expressions commonly used in interaction. For example, *certainly* often appears in the ALC to express agreement with an interviewee, but it is also as frequently employed in the corpus to emphasise the high probability of the speaker's beliefs (e.g. *painting today certainly seems very vibrant*). The tendency for this group of words to exhibit a decreasing trend in the ALC suggests that values of absoluteness or extremeness contribute more frequently to the conceptualisation of visual arts practice within the earlier decades of the corpus than they do in the later decades. In Table 20, for instance, which contains concordance lines from the 1950s and 1960s, the modal *must* is used to frame art practice as constituted by certain obligatory actions and values (*dealing with unconscious controls, being rational and objective*).

In the concordance lines in Table 21, *only* and *nothing* are employed by artists in a similar constitutive way. That is, they are used to make unconditional truth statements about the production or interpretation of art. The only indication of any qualification in these lines is the use of *I think* (lines 2 and 4). As always, all concordance lines are selected from different texts in the ALC.

As mentioned, the frequency of these types of emphatic and proclamatory statement substantially decline in the later decades of the corpus. The extent of this decline can be seen in Figure 10 which shows that the frequency of *must* decreased by 84 per cent from the 1950s until the 2010s. The figure also indicates the similar decrease of the modal *ought (to)*, which is also used to indicate obligation (Coates, 1983). Similarly, and although they do not occur in Table 9, the modal form *have (to)*, which like *must* also typically conveys extreme obligation, and the modal *should*, which can convey weak obligation,

Table 20 Selected concordance lines with *must* (1950s and 1960s)

1	arising from contemporary life. To make art the artist	must	deal with unconscious controls, the intuitive forces (1950)
2	to have rational association, but the act of painting	must	be rational, objective, and consciously disciplined (1950)
3	all, in the work itself. Just the same, the artist	must	say what he feels: My work grows from the duel (1950)
4	own painting as beautiful as I can. All theories	must	fall in the face of the fact of the painting (1960)
5	whole space. It is full of meaning, but the meaning	must	come from the seeing, not from the talking (1960)

Table 21 Selected concordance lines with *only* and *nothing* (1950s and 1960s)

1	object of his choice. Because of this, painting is the	only	art in which the intuitive qualities of the artistic may be (1950)
2	pieces are white because I think that white is the	only	colour that allows imaginary colour to be put on (1960)
3	more. They became exhibitionists. Art has	nothing	to do with exhibitions. That means too often dullness (1950)
4	I think that in abstract art, as there's no report, there's	nothing	other than the aesthetic of the painter and his few (1960)

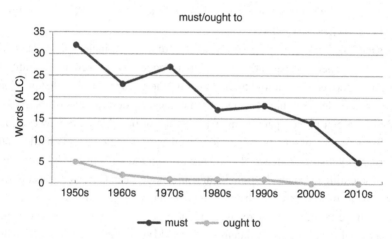

Figure 10 Frequency of *must* and *ought (to)* over time in the ALC

both exhibit a strong overall decrease in frequency throughout successive decades of the ALC.

Furthermore, and in contrast to the artists from the latter decades of the corpus, Table 22 shows that the artists of the 1950s and 1960s discursively conceptualise their art practice through the concepts of purity and truth.

These artists who made the statements in Table 22 are reproducing discourses that were widely prevalent at the time and were repeatedly found in the utterances of other artists. Matisse, for example, in an essay titled 'Exactitude is Not truth' produced for the catalogue of a 1948 exhibition of his works, stated that: [T]here is an inherent *truth* which must be disengaged from the outward appearance of the object to be represented. This is the only *truth* that matters' (Matisse, 1948: 33–4) and Cezanne, in a much earlier statement, proclaimed: 'I

Table 22 Selected concordance lines referring to purity and truth (1950s and 1960s)

1	art interest. I am looking for an essential	pure	image that is obviously derived from modern materials (1960)
2	is of a painting that declares this sensed reality in the	purest	and simplest terms the total painting as the image (1960)
3	an act of personal conviction and identity. If there is	truth	in art, it is his own truth. It is doubtful if aesthetics (1950)
4	future should therefore be very interesting. The	true	creative artist has a powerful urge and is not likely (1950)

owe you the truth [*vérité*] in painting and I will tell it to you' (Cezanne, 1905, cited in Danchev, 2013: 356).

As indicated in Section 1, the early decades of the ALC include the tail end of the historical period frequently referred to as modernity, as well as the cultural and social movement referred to modernism. There are many texts that provide considerably detailed, nuanced and often contesting descriptions of these two different, albeit related paradigms, and this is not possible here. However, in brief, modernity describes the period from approximately 1650 until 1950 where the totalising influence of the church was gradually replaced by individualism, scientific reason and rationalism, while modernism is viewed as a cultural and artistic movement, which from approximately 1880 until 1950 rejected prior artistic traditions (e.g. realism) as lacking the capacity to represent the advances taking place in the contemporary world at the time (Childs, 2017). The consequence was an ideological crisis that, in the art world, resulted the succession of a number of artistic movements in the early twentieth century, each of which engaged in distinctly different attempts to visually resolve what they perceived as the problem of representation, but which were also concerned with defending their particular artistic solutions. Importantly, this was often carried out through the types of aphorism or statement evidenced throughout this section.

The various artistic movements, in their attempt to respond to the crises of modernity embraced the representation of phenomena such as ephemerality, subjectivity and the unconscious. However, as indicated in the corpus extracts and quotations above, underlying these artistic foci was a concern with truth and absoluteness, both of which it could also be argued had an ideological connection to the ever increasing interest at the time in science. Such discourses are, as has been seen, evident in the statements of artists, and they ultimately inform their practices. For example, the early expressionist, Franz Marc wrote in his work *Aphorisms* (1914): '[T]he art to come will be giving form to our *scientific* convictions. This art is our religion, our centre of gravity, our *truth*' (Marc, 1914: 35, cited in Chipp, 1968: 180), while the pioneer abstractionist Piet Mondrian stated in an essay that: '[P]*ure* science achieves practical results for humanity. Similarly, one can say that *pure* art even though it appears abstract, can be of direct utility for life.' Mondrian goes on to say that: '[A]rt shows us that there are also *truths* concerning forms' (Mondrian, 1937: 45, cited in Chipp, 1968: 353; emphasis added).

3.6 Themes

According to Robertson and McDaniel (2017), art practice in the first decades of the twenty-first century involved a preoccupation with certain moral and ethical themes, which they state included 'political agency, spirituality, beauty, violence, sexuality, transience, extinction, memory and healing' (p. 31), as well as body, identity, science and time. Of these, it would appear that only *memory* is represented in the list of high frequency trending lemmas, exhibiting statistical significance in Table 6. Therefore, this section will focus in the first instance on the lemma *memory*, after which it will also examine the occurrence in the ALC of the other themes suggested by Robertson and McDaniel as more recently informing artists' creative practices.

The noun *memory* occurs sixty-one times in the ALC, exhibits the eighth strongest increasing trend of high frequency words in the corpus (1.38), and has a significant p-value of 0.035. Figure 11 illustrates the frequency of *memory* over time in the ALC. It can be seen that while the noun steadily increases in

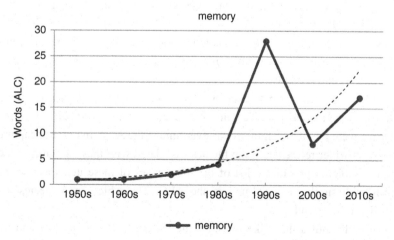

Figure 11 Frequency of *memory* over time in the ALC with trendline

frequency across the seven decades of the corpus, it also exhibits a considerable spike in the 1990s.

It is of interest to consider why *memory*, of all the lemmas representing the themes that shape visual artists' conceptualisation of their practices, exhibits the most significant increase over time in the ALC. Klein (2000) in his study of the emergence of the memory discourse states that a dramatic increase in the scholarly focus on *memory* as a key word began in the 1980s, particularly in the disciplines of literature, history and anthropology. He states that the word *memory* is now used synonymously with history, largely because it feels less distant or objective than history and is able to provide a stronger connection between the past and our own experiences. Similarly, Gibbons (2007) suggests that the increased preoccupation with memory in late twentieth century western culture is the result of the postmodern reshaping of memory from what was previously seen as something objective and immutable, to a phenomenon understood as subjective and relativist. She has stated that this shift in the conceptualisation of memory has provided creative individuals, in particular artists, with the opportunity to develop works that examine the connections between memory and culture. Furthermore, Huyssen (2012) suggests that the late twentieth-century obsession with memory is a reaction against the modernist emphasis on temporality and novelty. He argues that over time contemporary artists lost confidence in the future focussed avant-gardism of the early twentieth century and instead turned to 'the past and to history, to memory and remembrance' (p. 98).

Table 23 provides a selection of five concordance lines containing the lemma *memory* from the 2010 decade of the ALC. As can be seen in the table, the artists' explanations regarding the way that the theme of memory facilitates their practices closely aligns with the discussions above, including the description of the cultural concern with memory as an 'obsession' (Gibbons, 2007: 5; Huyssen 2012: 6), the conceptualisation of memory as an irrational and subjective experience, and the claim that art practice provides a vehicle for 'memory-work' (Gibbons, 2007: 5).

Of the other themes mentioned by Robertson and McDaniel as providing catalysts for creative practice, only the lemmas *body*, *politically*, *sex* and *violence* were found to exhibit trends over time in the ALC. In order to capture the artists wider reference to the themes associated with these lemmas in the corpus, Table 24 provides a list of the frequencies of these items as well as words with similar stems found in the ALC. The table also indicates the direction of the trend.

The table shows that, like *memory*, the themes of *body*, *politics* and, to a lesser degree, *sexuality* and *violence* exhibit an increase over time in the

Table 23 Selected concordance lines with the noun *memory* from the ALC
(1990s and 2010s)

1	he relationship between the subterranean *irrational*	memory	and the upper executive space of language, in other words (2010)
2	my work encourages viewers to draw **upon their own**	memories	and **experiences** when ·contemplating my work (2010)
3	I became **obsessed** with the mechanisms of	memories	and **I used them as subject matter for my paintings** (2010)
4	you're there in the moment, rather it feels like a	memory	with your **own filter of how** you felt about it. I like (2010)
5	terms of truth. But I want to open up the subject of	memory	as the **subjectivity of memory**, as the genealogy (1990)
6	very beginning my work has been **obsessed** with selective	memory.	In my early twenties **I produced a series of works that** (1990)

ALC. The other theme, mentioned by Robertson and McDaniel (2107), *time*, has an overall frequency of 636 in the ALC and is more or less equally distributed across the seven decades. However, because of myriad uses of *time* in the corpus, many of which are not related to the use of time as a thematic catalyst for art practice, it was excluded from the frequency counts in Table 24.

3.7 Language

Of the four lemmas semantically related to language that exhibit statistically significant trends in the ALC (Table 6), the noun *language* and the verb *read* exhibit an increase over time, while the nouns *word* and *statement* exhibit a decrease over time. Each of these lemmas will be discussed separately in the sectionsthat follow.

3.7.1 The Noun Language

Table 25 reproduces five of eighty-five concordance lines in the ALC that contain the noun *language*. They were selected from the 2000 decade, which had an unusually high occurrence of the noun, and provide a useful representation of its particular uses in the corpus.

Table 24 Frequency of certain themes (using related lexical items) over time in the ALC

Theme	Associated.lexis and total frequency	1950	1960	1970	1980	1990	2000	2010	Total	Trend
body	body (121), bodies (21), bodily (8), body-builder (1)	5	6	9	18	35	13	65	151	↑
politics	political (49), politic (16), politically (9), politicised (1), politicians (1)	8	2	2	7	17	19	21	76	↑
memory	memory (46), memories (15), memorial (3), memorable (2), memorials (1) memorise (1) memorably (1)	2	1	2	5	29	13	18	70	↑
sexuality	sexual (15), sex (14), sexuality (10), sexy (5), sexier (1), sexes (1)	0	0	1	11	18	10	6	46	↑
violence	violence (23), violent (9), violently (2)	1	3	2	3	4	12	9	34	↑

Table 25 Selected concordance lines with the noun *language* from the ALC (2000s)

1	about institutions and individuals with bodies,	languages	and histories. And some of the individuals and
2	or even the actual physical process, the **visual**	language	**of the marks** themselves? How can I continue to make
3	work with it. Unconsciously **we are creating a**	language	that another human being can pick up on. We connect
4	sacrificing much for the sake of the anger. Rough	language	and images meant to shock were often the driving
5	exploration and development. Finally, it is the	languages	**of figure painting** that attract me to the larger

Overall, it is evident that the noun *language* is used both metaphorically and literally in the ALC. In lines 2, 3 and 5, for example, *language* is used metaphorically. In line 2, the collection of marks made by the artist on the surface of the painting are conceptualised as components of a language, while in line 3, the artist constructs their work as involving the creation of a type of language. Similarly, in line 5, the artist also metaphorically constructs figure painting as a language (or given the plural, as a group of languages). In contrast, line 1 uses *languages* literally in reference to the specific language use of individuals or institutions, while the use of language in line 4 to refer to the inclusion of words as content in a painting is also literal. Following a qualitative examination of all instances of *language* in the ALC, Figure 12 provides a comparison of the frequencies over time of the noun *language* used metaphorically and literally in the ALC. The figure indicates that both the metaphoric and literal use exhibit an overall increase until the 2000s after which there is a decline. It also indicates a decline in the metaphoric use of *language* in the 1970s and a peak in its literal use in the same decade.

As indicated in Section 1.2.4, Sullivan (2009) also found that the metaphorical conceptualisation of art as communication was prevalent in the artists' statements that she analysed from a leading art magazine published between 2002 and 2003. The spike in the frequency of the lemma *language* in the ALC occurs in the same decade as that of Sullivan's data, which may suggest that her analysis focussed on a period when this metaphorical conceptualisation was particularly prominent – at least as characterised through the noun *language*. Interestingly, the frequency of the expression *visual language* (Table 25, line 2), which Sullivan also implies was particularly prevalent in her corpus, was found to occur five times in the ALC,

Table 26 Selected concordance lines with the verb *read* from the ALC (2000s)

1	of seducing-repelling. I don't want people to	read	**my work.** I want them to be in the presence of it and to (1960)
2	it be as a mother, lover, or daughter. I can usually	read	**the narrative** very clearly after the painting is complete (1990)
3	and phallus. I was more interested in a **statement** I	read	by Mondrian in which he spoke of putting down a red (1960)
4	In our culture, you get information all the time,	reading	**papers,** watching television. There is always (1990)

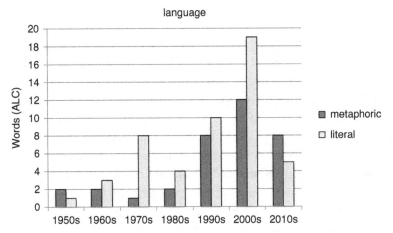

Figure 12 Metaphoric and literal uses of *language* in the ALC

once in the mid-1990s and four times in the 2000s. Again this is the same period as Sullivan's corpus.

3.7.2 The Verb Read

The verb *read* also exhibits a significant increase in frequency over time in the ALC and is found in the corpus to refer, first, to the interpretation of the constituent elements of a work of art and, second, to the reading of written texts related to, or placed directly in, the artwork. The former use can be seen the first two concordance lines in Table 26 from the ALC corpus, while the latter can be seen in the lines 3 and 4. In line 1, the artist distinguishes between the 'reading as interpretation' of a work (which elsewhere in the text, they explicitly

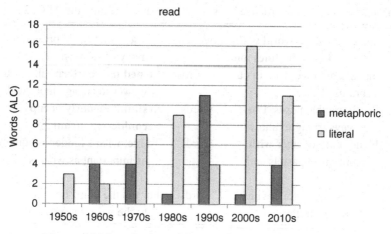

Figure 13 Metaphoric and literal uses of *read* in the ALC

state involves focussing on its component parts) and experiencing the work as a whole. In line 2, the artist conceptualises her work as containing a narrative that can be read both by herself, and her viewers. Not surprisingly, the characterisation of the constituent elements of a work of art as phenomena that can be metaphorically read, like words in a text, has a direct relationship to the metaphoric conceptualisation of art as a language discussed in Section 3.7.1.

Figure 13 compares the frequency of these two uses of *read* in the ALC. Interestingly, artists' literal reference to the texts they are reading within the context of their art practice steadily increases from the 1950s until it peaks in the 2000s. Conversely, the metaphorical use of *read*, however, exhibits little overall trend, although it does peak considerably in the 1990s.

3.7.3 The Noun Word

As shown in Figure 14, the frequency of the noun *word* significantly decreases in the ALC from the 1950s until the 2000s, after which it exhibits a sudden increase. However, thirty-five occurrences of all 162 occurrences of *word* in the ALC involved the expression *in other words*, the majority of which were found in the 1960s. The dotted line in Figure 14, therefore, indicates the frequencies over time of artists' use of the noun *word* excluding this expression. An examination of COHA also found that the 1960s had a considerably more frequent use of *in other words* than in successive decades. A closer inspection of the ALC also shows that, unlike *language* and *read*, *word* is never used metaphorically in the corpus.

The five concordance lines in Table 27 selected from the 2010 decade of the ALC provide an indication of the ways in which an artist in the later decades of the

Table 27 Selected concordance lines with the noun *word* from the ALC (2000s)

1	and **explore** the world **with the aid of some lines and**	words.	I'm sure this has happened to many of us. Basically, I
2	that are jumbled deep in our brains. These	'words	**turned into pattern**' allows the viewer to engage more with
3	the figure that poses. I'm always trying to allow	words	to **simultaneously occupy conflicting meanings**.
4	blend it all together **with** paint, inks, pastels and even	words.	To me, what's hidden is equally as important as what is
5	language its history, which comes from the	words.	For me the term 'fine art' refers to the work I create that is

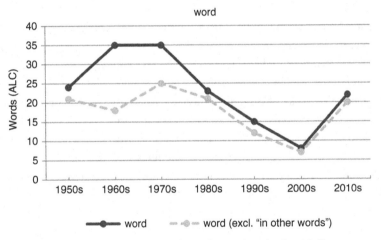

Figure 14 Frequency of *word* over time in the ALC

corpus conceptualises an engagement with words as a legitimate catalyst for their visual practice. In line 1 and 4, the artists simply refer to their work as containing the use of words. Line 1 also includes an example of the exploration discourse (Section 1.1) and the artist characterises the literal inclusion of words in their work as assisting with their 'exploration'. In line 2, the artists' work includes repetitive marks that they suggest are representative of words; a resemblance that it might be argued contributes to the artistic interest of the work. In line 3, the artists' works are motivated by wordplays, while in line 5 (although not explicitly clear from the concordance line itself), the artists' works are illustrations of words. Each of these lines, as usual, is selected from a different text in the 2010 decade.

In contrast, the use of the noun *word* by artists in the 1950s and 1960s decades of the ALC is most often used to construct the inadequacy of words (used metonymously here to represent language) for expressing the visual, or more specifically, for describing particular aspects of visual art. These uses are exemplified in the concordance lines in Table 28. Lines 1, 2 and 4 construct language as beyond the capabilities or requirements of the visual artist. In doing so they constitute the artist and their work as having a unique or exceptional visual ability, one that is not easily open to verbal description. Line 5 has a similar function, but focusses on the viewer's interpretation of the work. Furthermore, and reinforcing the conceptualisation of visual art as unique from language, lines 3, 6 and 7 make reference to particular words (*aesthetic, lyrical, transformation*) that the speaker constitutes as inadequate or problematic for the description of visual art. All concordance lines are selected from different texts in the ALC.

3.7.4 The Noun Statement

Although exhibiting peaks in the 1960s and the 1990s, the frequencies of the noun *statement* show an overall decline across the seven decades of the ALC

Table 28 Selected concordance lines with the noun *word* from the ALC (1950s and 1960s)

1	of others. **A painter should never speak** because	words	**are not the means at his command. Words cannot express visually** (1950)
2	And now I am approaching the territory where	words	**can hardly follow.** Taste and quality are as difficult to (1950)
3	as having 'real poetry'. Yet the alternative	word,	**'aesthetic'**, does not satisfy me. It calls up in (1950)
4	the energetic aspect of seeing. An artist's	words	**are always to be taken cautiously.** The finished (1950)
5	I don't think that when they look at an artwork they should be concerned with	words.	It should be visual: visual-emotional, not verbal emotional (1960)
6	if my pictures are more **'lyrical'** (that loaded	word!)	because I'm a woman. Looking at my paintings as (1960)
7	strength of Pop art. **Transformation** is a strange	word	to use. It implies that art transforms. It doesn't (1960)

(Figure 15). A qualitative examination of *statement* in the corpus indicates that of all fifty occurrences, three are used to specifically reference the artists' statement, eighteen refer to general statements about art or some other phenomenon and twenty-nine are specifically used to reference the artist's own visual work. This last use is of the most interest here, as it relates to the metaphoric construction of visual arts practice *as* language. Table 29, which provides a list of concordance lines from the ALC that function in this way, indicates that *statement* is often used as a synonym for (art)work. Artists, for example, conceptualise their practices as *making* statements (lines 1, 2, 5), or *presenting* statements (line 4). Surprisingly, only two of the lines in the table (5 and 6) constitute the statement/artwork as explicitly *about* some phenomenon. A further examination of the ALC reveals that of the fifty occurrences of *statement*, only seven collocate with *about*, perhaps suggesting that the metaphorisation of the artwork as a statement does not require the expected entailment of 'aboutness'; that is, the work is simply a statement. In line 3, the statement is constructed as existing *in* the work – the only example of this particular characterisation in the ALC – and following the discussion in the previous section, line 4 also explicitly constitutes the statement/artwork as something that is *readable*.

Table 29 Selected concordance lines with the noun *statement* from the ALC

1	to me was just something. I had **made** a very **formal**	statement;	I had put down something of what I had found in (1950)
2	artists have found new ways and new means of **making their**	statements.	Each age finds its own technique. Yes that always (1950)
3	divert you from its formal content. I think **the formal**	statement	**in my work** will become clearer in time. Superficially (1960)
4	**presenting** as simple, economical, and as wholly **readable** a	statement	as possible. But at the same time, I really don't know (1970)
5	For years I was trying to **make** general and objective	statements	**about** the state of the world. With Measures of (1990)
6	subtracting, until I ultimately commit to this particular	statement	**about** the landscape. After I commit, the completion of the painting (2010)

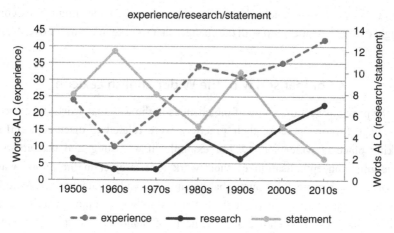

Figure 15 Frequency of *research, statement,* and *experience* over time in the ALC

An examination of texts in the later decades of the ALC indicate that conceptualisation of the artwork as an *experience* or as *research* has over time succeeded its conceptualisation as a *statement*. Figure 15 provides a comparison of the frequencies of these two nouns with that of *statement* and demonstrates that their use increases over the seven decades of the ALC, while *statement* declines. The reconceptualisation of art practice as *research* was discussed in Section 3.3.

To conclude, this section has analysed a number of lemmas statistically identified as exhibiting trends in the ALC corpus to provide an indication of how artists' conceptualisation of their creative practices may have changed from the beginning of the 1950s until the end of the 2010s. Prominent trends include the increasing conceptualisation of art practice as an engagement with the medium of the work, as well as the increasing projectification of the artists' creative activities, the latter of which includes a move towards a more audience-centred, conceptualisation of art. Artists have also internalised a wider range of verb processes from which to constitute their creative practices, although verbs such as *solve* or *eliminate*, previously used to construct art as the solution or elimination of a problem, have considerably decreased, as has artists' use of emphatic and proclamatory statements. The use of the concept *memory* as a catalyst for practice has also increased and the conceptualisation of art practice as a statement has been replaced by its conceptualisation as research or an experience.

Based on the view that the language used by artists to conceptualise their practices emerges from a wider social and historical context, the next stage of this Element seeks to establish whether changes in the wider English lexicon might exhibit a relationship with the changes that were found to occur over time in the ALC.

4 Comparison with the Wider English Lexicon

In the previous section, some of the changes in the way that artists have used language to conceptualise their practices were related to discursive shifts taking place in wider society. For example, it was suggested that artists' emerging conceptualisation of their work as a project in the 1990s was informed by a project discourse that began to pervade contemporary society around the same time (Cicmil et al., 2016). In another example, it was implied that artists' increasing choice of the concept of *memory* as a catalyst for their practices mirrored the wider social and scholarly preoccupation with memory, particularly its emergence as a synonym for history, in the late twentieth century (Gibbons, 2007). It was also suggested that society's escalating interest in new scientific discourses at the beginning of the twentieth century influenced the heightened concern that many artists had with truth, purity and absoluteness at the time. Importantly, the rise or decline of these wider social beliefs and discourses are manifest in everyday language use (Fairclough, 1992; Baker, 2006). For example, the Corpus of Historical American English shows a steady decline in the relative frequencies of the words *truth*, *pure* and *absolute* since the 1900s and a marked increase in the words *memory* and *project* in the late twentieth century. As a result, and in order to further evaluate the relationship between the types of discursive shift occurring over time in general English, and the language used by artists to conceptualise their practices, this section will statistically compare artists' words identified in the previous section as exhibiting diachronic trends over the seven decades of the ALC with their occurrence in COHA. The aim is to establish whether there is a statistical correlation between the diachronic changes of these words in the two corpora that might provide evidence that artists' changing conceptualisations of their practices, at least in the English-speaking context, are influenced by shifts in the wider lexicon. In light of the findings from the correlation analysis, the section will also provide a more detailed examination in COHA of some of the words identified as trending in the ALC, in an attempt to account for their increase or decrease over time in the ALC.

A preliminary example of a comparison between the ALC and COHA can be provided using the verb *connect*. The trend analysis in Section 3.4 found that there was a statistically significant increase in artists' use of the verb *connect* to conceptualise their creative practices in the ALC. Figure 16

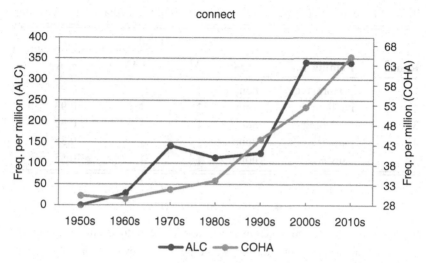

Figure 16 Frequency comparison of *connect* in the ALC and COHA

compares the frequencies of the verb *connect* across the seven decades of the ALC with those of COHA. As indicated in Section 2.3.2, raw word frequencies in this section have been normalised to 'frequency per million words' to enable the comparison. Also as indicated, the figure contains different scales for the y-axis (frequencies), but keeps the x axis (decades) aligned. While the use of dual scales can potentially misrepresent the precise relationship between two sets of data, for the purposes of this Element it provides a useful and accessible visual comparison of frequency trends over time. What is evident from Figure 16 is that the relative frequency of the verb *connect* in the ALC exhibits a similar trend to the relative frequency of the verb *connect* in COHA.

As indicated in Section 2.3.2, the relationship of a word or lemma's movement over time in the ALC and COHA can also be measured using the Pearson Product-Movement Correlation Coefficient. The coefficient produces values which range from 1 to −1. The closer a correlation score is to 1, the more closely related the movement of the lemma is between the two corpora, while the closer the score is to −1, the more inversely related the lemma is between the two corpora. Using the coefficient, the correlation score of the verb *connect* is 0.90, which, as suggested by Figure 16, indicates that the frequency distributions of the verb across the seven decades of the two corpora are very highly correlated suggesting, as discussed above, that this may be more than a coincidence. The following comparison between the ALC and COHA is organised using the same semantic groupings that structured the trend analysis in Section 3.

Table 30 Trend directions and correlation scores of the media and modes group

Rank[7]	Lemma	POS	Trend ALC	COHA	Correlation score
1	performance	noun	↑	↑	0.97
2	medium[8]	noun	↑	↑	0.93
3	technology	noun	↑	↑	0.62
4	painter	noun	↓	↓	0.38
5	canvas	noun	↓	↑	−0.58

4.1 Media and Modes

Table 30 shows the trend direction and correlation score for each of the nouns in the media and modes group for the two corpora.[6] It is evident that all nouns in the group, with the exception of *canvas*, trend in the same direction in the ALC as they do in COHA. Again, with the exception of *canvas*, they all exhibit a positive correlation score, with those of *performance* and *medium* indicating a very strong relationship between their movements over time in the two corpora. The noun *performance*, in particular, exhibits a correlation score of 0.97, the strongest of all trending lemmas listed earlier in Table 6. Therefore, it is of particular interest to see what appears to account for its increase in frequency in COHA, and how this might potentially align with its increase in the ALC.

Figure 17 provides a line graph which visually indicates the strong relationship of the movement of the noun *performance* over the seven decades of the two corpora. It can be seen that the noun exhibits a very steady increase from the 1970s onwards, with the exception of a slight decrease in the 2000s.

An examination of the items that collocate with performance in COHA from the 1820s to the 2010s (−4/+4, MI ≥ 3) suggests that the noun *performance* performs three primary semantic functions. The first involves the use of *performance* to refer to the completion of a *task* or *duties* (e.g. *the performance of his public duty*). This usage of *performance* to describe the fulfilment of what is required is etymologically linked to the fourteenth-century verb *performen* and its prominent usage in COHA appears to decline by the end of the nineteenth century. The second semantic function of *performance* in

---

[6] The direction of the trend for the ALC column is determined by the trend statistic in Sketch Engine. The direction of the trend in the COHA column was established by applying a linear trendline to the figures produced by the relative frequency statistics in Excel.

[7] Items in the tables in this section are ranked according to correlation.

[8] COHA does not include *media* as a lemma of *medium*, so the statistics for the noun *medium* were established by including the combined diachronic frequency results for the lemmas of the nouns *medium* and *media*.

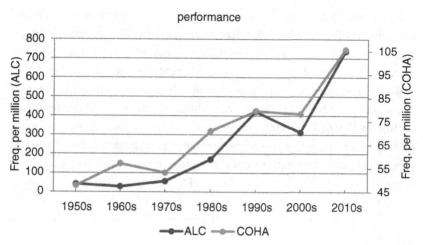

Figure 17 Frequency comparison of the noun *performance* in the ALC and COHA

COHA involves its usage to describe the creative act, typically of a musical or theatrical nature (e.g. *theatrical performance*). Etymologically, this usage of the noun is seen as emerging in the seventeenth century and in COHA its usage first peaks around the end of the nineteenth century. After a brief decline, however, it begins to increase in frequency again in the 1970s. The third and perhaps most interesting semantic function of *performance* refers more broadly to capability or competence and is increasingly evident in collocates such as *academic performance, economic performance, environmental performance* and even *sexual performance*. It is also potentially linked to emerging discourses of accountability and efficiency, which began to appear in the 1970s and are typically associated with rise of new public management and related practices such as the performance review (e.g. Parker, Jacobs and Schmitz, 2019). It is this broadening application of the noun performance and its subsequent availability for borrowing that arguably most contributes to its dramatic increase in frequency in COHA from the 1970s and which, I would suggest, has impacted on its increasing acceptance and use to describe practices beyond those associated with the theatre and classical music, such as performance art.

Interestingly, while art as performance has its historical origins earlier in the twentieth century, it was not until the 1970s that it was accepted as an art form in its own right (Goldberg, 2001). It has even been suggested that the 1970s can be viewed as the decade of performance (Damman, 2018), a period in which artists, among others, attempted to shift the term away from its more conventional theatrical use. Finally, performance studies, an interdisciplinary area that focuses on the centrality of performance in social and cultural life, was also formalised as an academic field during the 1970s. Overall, there is a sense that a wider discourse of performance began to emerge and expand within various different contexts from the 1970s onwards. The increasing prevalence of this discourse is evident in the texts of the ALC and has undoubtedly contributed to the statistically significant decline in the ALC of the noun *painter* and the associated noun *canvas*. *Canvas*, interestingly, is one of the few lemmas discussed in this study that exhibit a negative correlation between the two corpora. However, a search of concordance lines with *canvas* in COHA indicates that the medium is associated with bags, shoes, marquees, jackets and other items not related to the visual arts and that appear to have increased in popularity in the past decades.

4.2 Practice

In Section 3.3, the nouns *project* and *exhibition* were identified as displaying particularly strong increases in frequency across the seven decades of the ALC. Furthermore, the nouns *practice* and *viewer* were found to have a close semantic association with *project* in both the ALC and wider visual arts context. While *practice* and *viewer* did not occur in the ALC list of high frequency trending lemmas, they were nevertheless discussed as displaying considerable increases over time in the corpus. Table 31 shows the trend direction and correlation score for each of these four nouns. It can be seen that they all trend in the same direction in the ALC as they do in COHA and that they also all exhibit a strong correlation score.

An examination of the noun *project* in COHA can provide further insights into the relationship between the two corpora. Table 32 provides a list of the fifteen most frequent collocates of the noun *project* from the 1950s to the 2010s in COHA that had a mutual information score of 3 or higher. The collocates occurred either four places to the left or to the right of *project*.

Table 31 Trend directions and correlation scores of the practice group

| Rank | Lemma | POS | Trend | | Correlation score |
			ALC	COHA	
1	practice	noun	↑	↑	0.93
2	project	noun	↑	↑	0.88
3	viewer	noun	↑	↑	0.80
4	exhibition	noun	↑	↑	0.61

Table 32 Most frequent fifteen collocates of the noun *project* from the 1950s to the 2010s in COHA (+4/–4, MI ≥ 3)

Rank	Collocates	Freq.	MI
1	research	340	4.15
2	housing	267	5.98
3	complete	183	3.51
4	manager	172	4.01
5	construction	166	4.54
6	project	144	3.02
7	director	141	3.02
8	fund	136	3.26
9	science	126	3.11
10	ambitious	122	6.03
11	launch	110	3.81
12	finance	105	4.05
13	pilot	98	3.87
14	duration	87	6.22
15	propose	80	3.06

Table 32 provides a clear indication of the types of semantic group that the noun *project* is associated with in COHA. First, *complete, launch, pilot, duration* and *purpose* all semantically associate *project* with methodical planning and systematic organisation, a connection that is further supported by the collocates *manager* and *director*. In addition, the collocates *fund* and *finance* semantically associate *project* with financial matters. As indicated in Section 3.3, the ALC showed that from the 1950s to the 2010s, artists have increasingly constituted their creative work through the project discourse, as a planned, routinised and systematic practice. Interestingly, however, the most frequent collocate by some margin in Table 32 is *research* and again, as discussed in Section 3.3, this increasing conceptualisation of art practice as research is one of the more notable recent developments in the artworld. Figure 18 compares the frequencies over time of the noun *research* in the ALC with those of COHA and indicates that their trajectories are very closely aligned. *Research* also exhibits a strong correlation score of 0.85.

Finally, the occurrence of *science* in the most frequent *project* collocates from the 1950s to the 2010s in COHA is also of interest. A re-examination of the ALC indicates that the noun *science* occurs twenty-eight times from the 1950s to the 2010s, and suggests that discourses of science have

Table 33 Selected concordance lines with the noun *science* from the ALC (2000s and 2010s)

1	I just hitched a ride on science or not really	science	it was medicine. It's just collage, isn't it? Art is always very simple
2	Combining applied mathematics, computer	science,	and engineering, my work captures and freezes catastrophic
3	South America. This tome combines theology, natural	science,	and myth with maps, drawings, and descriptions of paradise
4	nature, but in collaboration with it. The images of	science,	for example photographs taken by the Hubble Space Telescope

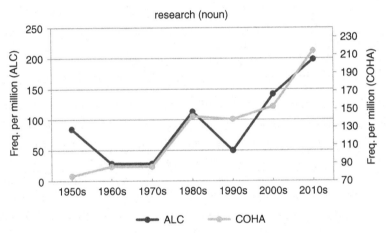

Figure 18 Frequency comparison of the noun *research* in the ALC and COHA

continued to maintain a presence in artist's conceptualisation of their practices. However, unlike the early modernist period where science in the visual arts was aligned with concerns of purity and truth (Section 3.5), science in the later decades of the ALC seems to provide a thematic or visual catalyst for the development of works. This is evidenced in the selected concordance lines from the 2000 and 2010 decades of the ALC (Table 33) and is also perhaps best observed in the sculptural works of the prominent British artist Damien Hirst, which have a philosophical and aesthetic preoccupation with science.

4.3 Constitutive Verbs

In Section 3.4, nineteen verbs used by artists to conceptualise their creative practices were identified as exhibiting a statistically significant increase across the seven decades of the ALC, while five exhibited a decrease.

In Table 34, it can be seen that of all twenty-four highest trending constitutive verbs only four, *resolve*, *strive*, *employ* and *inform* trend differently in the two corpora. Of the twenty verbs that trend in the same direction, six verbs, *capture*, *allow*, *explore*, *collect*, *construct* and *connect* are all very highly correlated, seven are highly correlated and one is moderately correlated. Overall, it is evident that the increase in the frequencies of the verbs used by artists to conceptualise their practices closely aligns with the increase in the frequencies of the same verbs in the wider English lexicon.

The verb *capture* received the highest correlation score in Table 34 (0.94), and a comparison of its frequencies across the seven decades of the ALC with those of COHA can be seen in Figure 19. The figure shows that from 1950 to 1970, *capture* does not occur at all in the ALC, however, from 1980, it displays a dramatic increase in use. With the exception of a slight dip in the 1990s, the verb displays a similar trajectory in the ALC. Etymologically, the verb *capture* has its origins in the Latin *capere*, which referred to the action of taking or seizing some tangible object (often an animal). However, *capture* has increasingly been used metaphorically and this usage is evident in the ALC where artists conceptualise their work as capturing some abstract phenomenon, such as an essence, a likeness or an imagination.

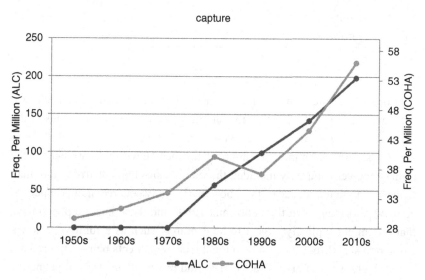

Figure 19 Frequency comparison of *capture* in the ALC and COHA

Table 34 Trend directions and correlation scores of the constitutive verb group

Rank	Lemma	POS	Trend direction		Correlation score
			ALC	**COHA**	
1	capture	verb	↑	↑	0.94
2	allow	verb	↑	↑	0.92
3	explore	verb	↑	↑	0.91
4	collect	verb	↑	↑	0.91
5	construct	verb	↑	↑	0.90
6	connect	verb	↑	↑	0.90
7	create	verb	↑	↑	0.86
8	combine	verb	↑	↑	0.85
9	challenge	verb	↑	↑	0.83
10	examine	verb	↑	↑	0.82
11	inhabit	verb	↑	↑	0.75
12	involve	verb	↓	↓	0.74
13	drive	verb	↑	↑	0.70
14	remind	verb	↑	↑	0.64
15	solve	verb	↓	↓	0.45
16	eliminate	verb	↓	↓	0.41
17	influence	verb	↑	↑	0.39
18	enjoy	verb	↑	↑	0.37
19	encourage	verb	↑	↑	0.35
20	free	verb	↓	↓	0.21
21	resolve	verb	↓	↑	−0.43
22	strive	verb	↑	↓	−0.53
23	employ	verb	↑	↓	−0.55
24	inform	verb	↑	↓	−0.76

In order to further examine the alignment between the verb *capture* in the ALC and COHA, Table 35 lists the ten most frequent noun collocates of the verb in the 1850s and 1990s, as well as in each decade from the 1950s to the 2010s. The search included nouns that appeared within four places to the right of the verb and only included those collocates that occurred more than twice in a particular decade. It can be seen that only concrete nouns appear as collocates of *capture* in the 1850s and 1900s and these include phenomena that one might typically expect to be captured, such as a fugitive, a town, a dog or a seal. From the 1950s to the 2010s, the objects being captured are increasingly those of an abstract nature, and by the 2010s, the only concrete noun collocate is *individual*. A cursory search of *capture/individual*

Table 35 Top ten noun collocates of the verb *capture* (0/+4, min. freq. 2, MI ≥ 0)[9] in COHA compared with all noun collocates of *capture* in the ALC (0/+4, MI ≥ 0)

Decade	COHA	ALC
1850s	fugitive, president, man, blount[10]	
1900s	vessel, food, water, dog, town, seal, mademoiselle, gun, girl, gang	
1950s	island, seat, imagination, **attention**, control, bridge, food, nation, mood, thing	
1960s	man, imagination, market, **attention**, control, party, nomination, ship, support, vessel	
1970s	woman, wonder, **attention**, imagination, energy, championship, share, life, initiative, wind	
1980s	**attention, essence, moment** imagination, business, city, child, reality, **image,** share	**essence**, appearance
1990s	spirit, **essence**, insect, film, light, flavour, share, electron, flag, data	**moment** (x2), rage, time
2000s	**attention, moment**, imagination, soul, spirit, city, **image**, market, complexity, people	**attention**, belief, world, expression, star
2010s	**moment, image, attention**, heterogeneity, light, effect, detail, preference, perspective, individual	dream (x2), **image** (x2), sketch experience, likeness, body

concordance lines, however, shows that these largely refer to the capturing of abstract concepts, such as an individual's *faith*, *propensity* and *experience*, among others. Of course, and as seen in the table, a few abstract nouns (i.e. *attention* and *imagination*) have been semantically associated with capture for some decades.

On the right-hand side of Table 35, the noun collocates with *capture* found in the ALC are listed relevant to their respective decade and those occurring in both the ALC and COHA columns are identified in bold. What is apparent is that

---

[9] In Table 4.6, a lower MI was necessary as the number of collocates with *capture* was small, especially in the earlier decades of the two corpora.

[10] The word *blount* is a reference to the capture of General Blount in a fictional work titled *Border War: A Tale of Disunion*, published by J.B. Jones in 1859.

there is a relationship between the appearance of these collocates in the ALC and in their appearance in COHA, perhaps suggesting that the shifting semantic association of these collocates provides new ways for discursively conceptualising artistic practice. Given the increasing familiarity of these collocates with the general user of English, it might be added that their use by artists to conceptualise their work is also likely to be accepted by their audiences (also see the discussion of *explore* in Section 2.3.4)

Section 3.4.1 identified five constitutive verbs whose frequencies over time in the ALC exhibited a decreasing trend. These verbs were *resolve, free, eliminate, solve* and *involve*. It was suggested that of these decreasing constitutive verbs, all but *involve* semantically functioned to describe the artist's work as an act against some undesirable phenomenon, for example a problem, dilemma or a concern. As seen in Table 34, four of the decreasing constitutive verbs also exhibited a decreasing trend in COHA. Of these, *involve* exhibits a high correlation between the two corpora, *eliminate* and *solve* exhibit a low correlation, while *free* shows very little correlation. In contrast, the verb *resolve* trends in opposite directions. Interestingly, a closer examination of the verb *solve* indicates that even lemmas with a low correlation score still demonstrate some periods of alignment across the two corpora.

Figure 20 compares the frequencies of the verb *solve* across the seven decades of the ALC with those of COHA. While in COHA, *solve* demonstrates an unusually dramatic increase in the 2010s, it is also apparent that from the 1950s to the 2000s the verb exhibited a similar overall downward trajectory in the ALC as it did in COHA. Indeed, even in the 2010s, the slight increase in its usage in the ALC reflected, albeit less strongly, its increase in COHA

Twelve of all eighteen occurrences of *solve* in the ALC involved a collocate with the noun *problem*. Figure 21 compares the frequency distribution of these *solve/problem* collocates with those occurring in COHA and a similar trajectory can also be observed. The *solve/problem* collocates in the two corpora have a high correlation score of 0.87.

4.4 Absoluteness and High Modality

Section 3.5 analysed a group of thirteen lemmas in the ALC that were all identified as having a semantic association with the expression of absoluteness or high modality. These lemmas were discussed as being employed by artists in the early decades of the ALC to either construct art practice as constituted by certain obligatory actions and values or to make

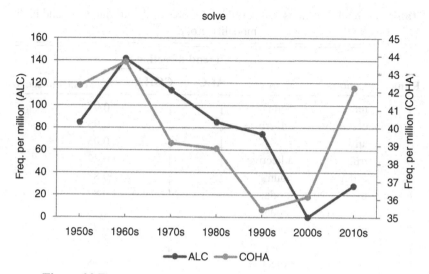

Figure 20 Frequency comparison of *solve* in the ALC and COHA

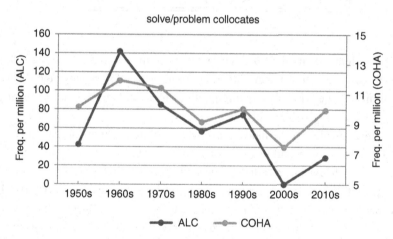

Figure 21 Frequency over time of the collocate *solve/problem* in the ALC and COHA

unconditional truth statements about the production or interpretation of art. Importantly, it was shown that each of these thirteen lemmas exhibited a significant decrease in frequencies across the seven decades of the ALC. Table 36 compares the trend direction of the frequencies for this group and shows that twelve of the thirteen lemmas also exhibit a decline in frequencies across the same seven decades of COHA. The table also provides the correlation score of the lemmas in this group and shows that nine of the

Table 36 Trend directions and correlation scores of the absoluteness and high modality group

Rank	Lemma	POS	Trend direction		Correlation score
			ALC	COHA	
1	unity	noun	↓	↓	0.97
2	certainly	adverb	↓	↓	0.95
3	any	-	↓	↓	0.95
4	true	adjective	↓	↓	0.87
5	order	noun	↓	↓	0.83
6	must	modal	↓	↓	0.82
7	ought (to)	modal	↓	↓	0.79
8	nothing	pronoun	↓	↓	0.77
9	none	pronoun	↓	↓	0.75
10	pure	adjective	↓	↓	0.68
11	full	adjective	↓	↓	0.66
12	no	-	↓	↓	0.48
13	only (adj)	adjective	↓	↑	−0.64

thirteen lemmas exhibit a high or very high correlation. Again, this reinforces the finding that the more prominent of the language trends identified in the ALC closely align with changes in language use occurring in the wider English lexicon.

An examination of the modal *must*, which exhibits a high correlation score (0.82), provides a useful example of the relationship between changes in the wider English lexicon and artists' conceptualisation of their practices. Figure 22 compares the frequencies over time of the modal *must* in the ALC and COHA. It can be seen that, although *must* was used relatively more frequently in the ALC in the 1950s, from the 1960s onwards the modal exhibits a similar downward trajectory in the two corpora.

In their corpus study of diachronic change in contemporary English, Leech et al. (2009) find that from 1961 to 1991 there was a significant and consistent decline in the overall use of modal auxiliaries, with both *must* and *ought (to)* displaying some of the more notable losses at 31.2 per cent and 37.5 per cent respectively. Similarly Baker (2017) shows a marked decline in the modal *must* from the 1930s until the 2010s. Both Leech et al. and Baker suggest that a potential reason for this decline may be a trend for democratisation, that is, speakers throughout the twentieth century and beyond have increasingly tended to avoid deontic language forms, such as *must* and *ought (to)* which can express

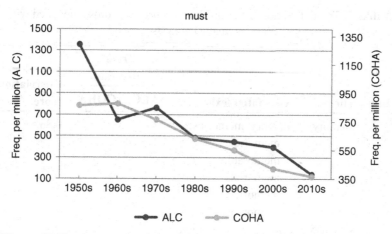

Figure 22 Frequency over time of the modal *must* in the ALC and COHA

an overly authoritarian or face-threatening stance (see also Leech, 2004). As indicated in Section 3.5, a concordance analysis of *must* from the 1950s and 1960s in the ALC shows that it is frequently used by artists to constitute art practice as involving certain obligatory actions and values (i.e. *the artist must say what he feels*). However, it was also shown that the use of these deontic statements significantly declines in the ALC from the 1950s to the 2010s. The comparison with COHA suggests that this decline is possibility shaped by the wider trend for democratisation.

4.5 Themes

Section 3.6 focused on the themes (memory, sexuality, body, violence and politics) that were identified as increasingly employed by artists in the ALC as thematic catalysts for their creative practices. Table 37 compares the trends of the groups of words associated with these themes in the ALC and the same related groups of words in COHA. The table also indicates their respective correlation scores. It shows that the groups associated with the themes of memory and sexuality exhibit a high positive correlation, while the group associated with body exhibits a moderate positive correlation. The table also shows that the theme of politics trends in opposite directions across the two corpora and has a very high inverse correlation.

A brief examination of the noun *memory* in COHA can account for its rise in frequency and change in usage over time and also provide insights as to its increasing use in the ALC to discuss socio-cultural concerns and subjective experiences (see Section 3.6). Table 38 compares a list of the top fiteen adjective + *memory* collocates in the ALC from the 1950s and the 2010s. In the 1950s, the

Table 37 Trend directions and correlation scores of words associated with thematic catalysts

Rank	Theme	Associated lexis	Trend direction ALC	Trend direction COHA	Correlation score
1	memory	memory, memories, memorial, memorable, memorials, memorize, memorably	↑	↑	0.83
2	sexuality	sexual, sex, sexuality, sexy, sexier, sexes	↑	↑	0.72
3	body	body, bodies, bodily, body-builder	↑	↑	0.68
4	violence	violence, violent, violently	↑	↑	0.35
5	politics	political, politic, politically, politicized, politicians	↑	↓	−0.91

most frequent adjectives that collocate with memory mostly describe the quality of an individual's memory (*good, poor, excellent, faulty, clear*). The only two exceptions are *recent* and *distant* in twelfth and nineteenth place respectively, both of which explicitly reference memory as a phenomenon associated with the past. In contrast, in the 2010s, six of the first ten collocates explicitly associate memory with the past; notably including the sixth highest collocate *historical memory*. What is also of interest is the appearance in the 2010s of adjectives such as *collective, human, cultural* and *social* in the top twenty adjective + *memory* collocates, which semantically conceptualise memory as a social-cultural phenomenon.

As discussed in Section 3.6, partly due to its connotations of subjectivity, the concept of memory began to replace the more objective concept of history from about the 1980s (Klein, 2000) and as a result began to appear as a key focus in a number of disciplines, including the visual arts where it was frequently employed to examine connections between memory and culture (Gibbons, 2007). Table 38, which shows the increasing semantic association of memory with history and culture, clearly supports these observations. The reconceptualisation of memory as a collective rather than individual reconstruction also

Table 38 Top fifteen adjective + *memory* collocates in COHA (1950s and 2010s, 1 L, MI ≥ 0)

	COHA 1950s				COHA 2010s		
Rank	adjective + *memory*	Freq.	Freq. per mil.	Rank	adjective + *memory*	Freq.	Freq. per mil.
1	good memory	20	0.70	1	recent memory	43	1.21
2	bad memory	9	0.31	2	good memory	30	0.85
3	long memory	8	0.28	3	short-term memory	22	0.62
4	photographic memory	5	0.17	4	distant memory	21	0.59
5	living memory	5	0.17	5	collective memory	19	0.54
6	poor memory	5	0.17	6	historical memory	19	0.54
7	excellent memory	4	0.14	7	photographic memory	19	0.54
8	faulty memory	4	0.14	8	long-term memory	12	0.34
9	vivid memory	4	0.14	9	favourite memory	11	0.31
10	loving memory	3	0.10	10	earliest memory	11	0.31
11	clear memory	3	0.10	11	affective memory	9	0.25
12	recent memory	3	0.10	12	bad memory	9	0.25
13	remarkable memory	3	0.10	13	human memory	9	0.25
14	retentive memory	3	0.10	14	cultural memory	8	0.23
15	short memory	3	0.10	15	old memory	8	0.23
16	sudden memory	3	0.10	16	social memory	8	0.23
17	unpleasant memory	3	0.10	17	spatial memory	8	0.23
18	wonderful memory	3	0.10	18	vivid memory	8	0.23
19	distant memory	2	0.07	19	new memory	7	0.20
20	dim memory	2	0.07	20	relational memory	7	0.20

aligns with the rise in artists' focus on their viewers' memories and experiences (Section 3.3.2); that is, an increased sense of themselves as 'speaking' for society. It is of interest that, mirroring the trends in the second column of Table 38, the words *collective, human* and *socially* exhibit upward trend scores in the ALC of 1.96, 2.36 and 3.49 respectively, while *historical* has an upward trend score of 1.8.

4.6 Language

Section 3.7 focused on artists' use in the ALC of the four lemmas, *language, read, word* and *statement* to conceptualise their creative practices. It was shown that the noun *language* and the verb *read* both exhibited an increase over time in the ALC, while the nouns *word* and *statement* both exhibited a decrease over time. As indicated in Table 39, the downward trend of *word* and *statement* in the ALC correlates with its trend in COHA, while *language* and *read* both exhibit negative correlation scores, even though the noun *language* trends upwards in both corpora. This is because, although trending upward, the relative frequencies of *language* across the two corpora tended to fluctuate in opposite directions from the 1980s onwards.

It was stated in Section 3.7.1 that the use of the expression *visual language* had five occurrences in the ALC, once in the mid-1990s and four times in the 2000s, and that this coincided with Sullivan (2009), who found a similar metaphorical conceptualisation of visual art as language in her study of artist's statements published between 2002 and 2003 (see Section 1.2). It is also of note that when the frequency of *visual language* was examined in COHA, it exhibited a similar pattern to the ALC, that is, it suddenly peaks in the 1990s after being absent in the corpus for many decades beforehand (Figure 23). Taking this into account with the findings in Section 3.7.1, there is some evidence for the suggestion that the metaphoric conceptualisation of art as a language was especially prominent around the turn of the twenty-first century.

Table 39 Trend directions and correlation scores of the language group

			Trend direction		
Rank	**Lemma**	**POS**	**ALC**	**COHA**	**Correlation score**
1	word	noun	↓	↓	0.76
2	statement	noun	↓	↓	0.57
3	read	verb	↑	↓	−0.23
4	language	noun	↑	↑	−0.27

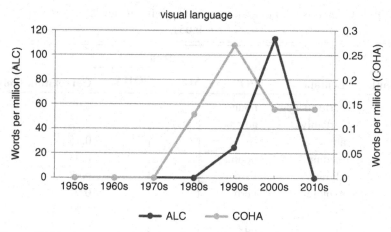

Figure 23 Frequency comparison of *visual language* in the ALC and COHA

The decline in frequency of the noun *statement* is also of interest and an examination of its usage in COHA may help account for its declining usage in the ALC where it was initially used to metaphorise the artist's visual work as a type of verbal declaration or announcement. In COHA, seven of all eight synonyms of the noun *statement*, as identified by the Cambridge Dictionary online, i.e. *announcement, remark, declaration, observation, pronouncement, proclamation* and *utterance*, also exhibit a marked overall decline in relative frequency since the 1950s (although *announcement* and *comment* do display a slight increase in the 2010s). This perhaps suggests that the use of lexis typically used to describe phenomena that express opinion are in overall decline. Indeed, even the noun *opinion* shows an overall 54 per cent decrease in COHA from the 1950s to the 2010s, and surprisingly an 84 per cent decrease in frequency from the 1820s to the 2010s. Furthermore, and as also found in the ALC (see Figure 15), the nouns *information* and *research* both of which were identified as replacing the conceptualisation of the artwork as a statement, also show a very considerable increase over time in COHA. It could be argued that the declining synonyms of *statement*, e.g. *announcement* and *remark*, represent individual activity and personal opinion, while *information* and *research* characterise collective activity, which aligns with the earlier discussion indicating a shift in artists conceptualisations of their practices from the individual and personal to the collective and social.

4.7 Overall Alignment

To conclude this section, Table 40 compares the trend direction of the twenty-eight high frequency lemmas that were found to exhibit a significant trend in

Table 40 Comparison of overall trends of high frequency lemmas (freq. ≥ 50, p < 0.05)

Rank	Lemma	POS	Trend		Correlation score
			ALC	COHA	
1	performance	noun	↑	↑	0.97
2	certainly	adv.	↓	↓	0.95
3	any	-	↓	↓	0.95
4	medium	noun	↑	↑	0.93
9	allow	verb	↑	↑	0.92
6	explore	verb	↑	↑	0.91
7	bit	noun	↑	↑	0.91
8	also	adv.	↑	↑	0.89
5	project	noun	↑	↑	0.88
10	actually	adv.	↑	↑	0.88
18	choose	verb	↑	↑	0.88
11	true	adj.	↓	↓	0.87
12	create	verb	↑	↑	0.86
14	order	noun	↓	↓	0.83
15	must	modal	↓	↓	0.82
13	memory	noun	↑	↑	0.77
17	nothing	pron.	↓	↓	0.77
16	word	noun	↓	↓	0.76
22	involve	verb	↓	↓	0.74
19	technology	noun	↑	↑	0.62
20	exhibition	noun	↑	↑	0.61
21	statement	noun	↓	↓	0.57
23	no	-	↓	↓	0.48
24	painter	noun	↓	↓	0.38
27	read	verb	↑	↓	−0.23
25	language	noun	↑	↑	−0.27
26	canvas	noun	↓	↑	−0.58
28	only (adj)	adj.	↓	↑	−0.64

Sketch Engine with their overall trend direction in COHA from the 1950s to the 2010s inclusive. The table also provides the correlation score for each lemma, established by comparing the frequencies over time for each of the seven decades of the two corpora. The twenty-eight lemmas in the table are ranked according to their respective correlation scores. It can be seen that of the twenty-eight lemmas, seven are very highly correlated (between 0.9 and 1.0), twelve are highly correlated (between 0.7 and 0.9) and three are moderately correlated (between 0.5 and 0.7). Only two exhibit a low correlation (between 0.3 and 0.5) and only four show a negative correlation. These results clearly indicate that the more significant trends in the language used by artists in the seven decades of the ALC generally tend to align with those found in COHA. The conclusions that can be drawn from these findings and its implications for future research will be discussed in the next section.

5 Discussion

The main conclusion that might be drawn from this study is that the language that artists draw on to both conceptualise their creative practices and rationalise these practices to their audiences is, in part, informed by the shifting trends that occur over time in everyday language use. For example, as certain verbs appear more frequently in everyday usage (e.g. *explore, challenge*) they are also likely to become part of the lexicon that contemporary artists draw on, albeit often unconsciously, as catalysts for their works. Or similarly, as certain nouns that reconceptualise phenomena in certain ways (e.g. as a *practice* or a *project*) become prevalent in everyday language, then it is likely that the wider discourses with which they are associated will also impact the way that artists perceive the nature of their creative activity. Or furthermore, as the use of lexis associated with certainty or obligation diminishes in everyday life, then the impact of these traits on the way that artists conceptualise what they, and other artists do, is also likely to decline.

Of course, artists as members of the wider community will also contribute to changes in the general lexicon and there are instances where shifts in artists' use of certain specialist art terms have impacted on their occurrence in wider usage; for example, the decline of the noun *painter* in COHA most likely mirrors its decline in the art world. However, it is highly unlikely that artists as a community are uniquely responsible for the type of wider language shifts discussed in this Element, such as the emergence of the project or memory discourse, the decline of lexis associated with certainty and obligation or the language shifts associated with democratisation and so on. Nevertheless, the community of artists do augment the changes in the language that they ultimately draw on to conceptualise their practices as they are inevitably influenced by reading and listening to one another's accounts of their work. Importantly, while the findings of this element provide explicit linguistic evidence that support the historical observations of Harris (2003) that certain discourses, which he refers to as 'artspeak', have influenced the practices of artists, it also shows that these constitutive discourses are far broader than those specifically related to the contexts of art practice and are widely pervasive in general language. It also shows that these discursive influences typically involve smaller scale language features, for example, the increase or decline in the use of certain modals, verbs or adverbs.

Diachronic corpus scholarship has attempted to identify what has facilitated everyday changes in language use. In addition to democratisation, discussed earlier, Leech (2004) suggests that language change is affected by colloquialisation (or informalisation) (that is, the tendency for the characteristic features of spoken language to increasingly pervade the written language) and 'Americanisation', the influence of specifically American expression to influence other dialects and languages. Baker (2017) adds to these densification; that is, the increasing tendency towards shorter units of communication and grammaticalisation, the increasing behaviour of lexical items as grammatical constructions (e.g. *going to*). Of these, democratisation appears to impact most strongly on the shifts found in the language used by artists to describe their work and, as indicated, can be most evidenced in the decreasing trends found in the semantic category of absoluteness and high modality (Sections 3.5 and 4.4). However, democratisation is also viewed as related to inclusion and group membership (Baker, 2017) and hence may also have an impact on the way that certain word trends, rather than others (for example, the particular constitutive verbs identified in Section 3.4) become part of the lexicon used by contemporary artists as catalysts for their works. There is a long history of artists forming in-groups that are motivated towards similar creative practices and who also noticeably use similar language to conceptualise their artworks. As Leech (2004) also points out, the self-identification with a social group can be responsible for the expansion of certain language forms into the wider usage of the group and he links this linguistic process to the social-psychological theory of accommodation. One notable example of accommodation in visual arts language is perhaps artists' increasing use in the late twentieth century of words associated with the translations of French theory (Rule and Levine, 2012; Lejeune et al., 2013). Rule and Levine include the words *field* and *transforms* as examples of this practice, both of which exhibit increasing trends in the ALC. However, I would argue that rather than being a superficial appendage to an artist's practice, as suggested by Rue and Levine, such language is facilitative of artistic work. The artists' conceptualisation of their work as a *transformation* of some phenomena, for example, has become over time a legitimate motivation for their visual practice and simultaneously has come to provide the viewer with a framework for interpretation.

Nevertheless, and as indicated throughout this Element, the most significant influence on shifting trends in the language used by artists is arguably the emergence of certain wider social and cultural discourses. Those having the most noticeable impact on the artists represented in the ALC and evidenced in the decline of language associated with absoluteness, high modality and purity (Section 3.5) are postmodern discourses related to the rejection of absolutes, binary oppositions and historical metanarratives. The impact of these discourses might include a widening of the types of medium and mode used by artists, as well as the particular type of motivations established for deploying this range of ever increasing media (Section 3.2). Other discourses identified as facilitating language shifts in the ALC are those related to the corporate world. These shape the conceptualisation of the artists' practice as a project, where outcomes are increasingly perceived as predetermined and agency is shifted to the audience as client. They also perhaps facilitate the increased emphasis of artistic practice on the exhibition of work (Section 3.3). Finally, the focus on concerns of memory, can be viewed as a response to the postmodern discourses of historical objectivity (Section 3.6), while the conceptualisation of art as a language might be understood, at least in part, as a response to the increasing acceptance of semiotic discourse that constructs images as phenomena that are able to be 'read' (Section 3.7).

While discourses emerge to influence change in artists' language and the conceptualisation of their creative practices, older discourses are not necessarily discarded. In Section 1, for example, it was discussed that discourses of nature and beauty shaped early art practices and that these were replaced by modern discourses associated with exploration and study. Interestingly, however, the lexis associated with nature and beauty discourses remains stable across the seven decades of the ALC, and items associated with exploration discourses continue to exhibit an increase in usage. In contrast, the occurrence in the ALC of lexis related to study discourses, which as I suggested were fundamental to the motivations of the early modernist painters, is more marginal. The noun *study*, for example, has an average frequency of three across the seven decades of the ALC, although it does exhibit a slight increase from the 2000s. It could be argued then, that art-facilitating discourses, although emergent at different historical periods, are not exclusive to one another and will be variously drawn on by artists at different times to shape their practices in diverse ways. Nevertheless, as suggested by this study, certain, often newly emergent, discourses are more prominent than others within certain periods and this is perhaps why similar kinds of contemporary art practice (often described as 'movements') appear during particular decades. I would also suggest that those institutions close to the nuclei of the contemporary art world, for example, certain galleries, art schools or prominent publications, are likely to champion certain prominent art discourses at any one time and will, ultimately, inform or sanction the creative practices of those individuals aligned with these institutions. Those artistic practices not conceptualised through the language of certain trending discourses may ultimately be overlooked by the important art institutions.

However, this is not to say that an artist's creativity is stifled or artistic conformity is enforced by discourse. As I have argued elsewhere, creativity itself is a discursive construct and varies according to social and historical context (Hocking, 2010, 2018). Indeed, in some areas, e.g. dance, hip-hop and classical music, creativity is characterised through repetition, as opposed to novelty (e.g. Danto, 1994; Pennycook, 2007), while a number of creativity scholars suggest that constraint is essential for creativity and show how artistic practice emerges as a result of the barriers imposed on artists (e.g. Johnson-Laird, 1988; Stokes, 2006). It could be argued, therefore, that those discourses perhaps viewed as constraining artists are in fact facilitative of their creative practices. Interestingly, as a discourse itself, creativity, or the act of being creative, has not always existed as a motivation for artistic practice. The first recorded use of the noun *creativity* was not until 1875 and only came into common usage in the 1940s. Neither does the word appear in COHA until 1890. As was discussed in Section 1.1, rather than being 'creative', it was the desire to visually study the natural object that motivated the artistic practices of the early modernists, not unlike the way in which a geologist is motivated to scientifically study a geological phenomenon.

5.1 Implications for Future Research

This exploratory study presents possibilities for future research. While the benefits of working with relatively small, specialised corpora were explained in Section 2.2, a larger corpus of artists' language would provide more general-isable findings and might level out the peaks and troughs that could be observed in the frequency counts of certain lemmas over time in the ALC. Similarly, while COHA is both the largest and most widely used diachronic corpus in the English language, future research might consider including other diachronic corpora for the comparison. There is also the potential for the results of this study, which focussed on texts produced in English, to be compared with the findings of similar research in other languages. Moreover, the results of this study could imply that the diachronic trends of items in other specialised corpora may follow those found in everyday language, suggesting that there is a closer relationship than often thought between specialised languages and the wider everyday lexicon, an implication that might warrant further investigation. Finally, it might be considered in greater depth whether, and to what degree, a corpus analysis can identify points in time where discourses change, merge or even come into conflict.

References

Adamson, N. and Goddard, L. (2012). Introduction. Artists' statements: Origins, intentions, exegesis. *Forum for Modern Language Studies* 48 (4), 363–75.

Alberti, L. B. (2011). De Pictura. In R. Sinisgalli (ed. & trans.), *Leon Battista Alberti: On Painting: A New Translation and Critical Edition*. Cambridge: Cambridge University Press, pp. 17–85. (Original work published 1435.).

Allpress, B., Barnacle, R., Duxbury, L. and Grierson, E. (2012). Supervising practice-led research by project in art, creative writing, architecture and design. In B. Allpress, R. Barnacle, L. Duxbury and E. Grierson (eds.), *Supervising Practices for Postgraduate Research in Art, Architecture and Design*. Rotterdam: Sense Publishers, pp. 1–14.

Aston, G. (1997). Small and large corpora in language learning. In B. Lewandowska-Tomaszczyk and P. J. Melia (eds.), *PALC '97: Practical Applications in Language Corpora*. Lódz: Lódz University Press, pp. 51–62.

Baker, P. (2006). *Using Corpora in Discourse Analysis*. London: Continuum.

Baker, P. (2011). Times may change but we'll always have money: A corpus driven examination of vocabulary change in four diachronic corpora. *Journal of English Linguistics* 39, 65–88.

Baker, P. (2017). *American and British English: Divided by a Common Language*. Cambridge: Cambridge University Press.

Baker, P., Gabrielatos, C. and McEnery, T. (2013). *Discourse Analysis and Media Attitudes: The Representation of Islam in the British Press*. Cambridge: Cambridge University Press.

Banaji, S., Burn, A. and Buckingham, D. (2010). *The Rhetorics of Creativity: A Review of the Literature*. Newcastle upon Tyne: Creativity, Culture and Education.

Barthes, R. (1967). The death of the author. *Aspen: The Magazine in a Box 5+6*. www.ubu.com/aspen/aspen5and6/threeEssays.html#barthes.

Belshaw, M. (2011). Artists' statements: The fate of the name. *Word & Image* 27 (1), 124–33.

Blunden J. (2020). Adding 'something more' to looking: The interaction of artefact, verbiage and visitor in museum exhibitions. *Visual Communication* 19(1), 45–71.

Bowker, L. and Pearson, J. (2002). *Working with Specialized Language: A Practical Guide to Using Corpora*. London: Routledge.

Brezina, V. (2018). *Statistics in Corpus Linguistics: A Practical Guide*. Cambridge: Cambridge University Press.

Childs, P. (2017). *Modernism*. Abingdon, UK: Routledge.

Chipp, H. B. (1968). *Theories of Modern Art: A Source Book by Artists and Critics*. Berkeley: University of California Press.

Cicmil, S., Lindgren, M. and Packendorff, J. (2016). The project (management) discourse and its consequences: On vulnerability and unsustainability in project-based work. *New Technology Work and Employment* 31(1), 58–76.

Clear, J. (2011). Corpus sampling. In G. Leitner (ed.), *New Directions in English Language Corpora*. Berlin: De Gruyter Mouton, pp. 21–32.

Coates, J. (1983). *The Semantics of Modal Auxiliaries*. London: Croom Helm.

Cunningham, K. J. (2019). Functional profiles of online explanatory art texts. *Corpora* 14 (1), 31–62.

Damman, C. (2018). Unreliable narrators: Laurie Anderson, Julia Heyward, and Jill Krosen perform the 1970s. In E. K. Usui (ed.), *Centre 38*. Washington, DC: National Gallery of Art, pp. 105–107.

Danchev, A. (2013). *The Letters of Paul Cézanne*. London: Thames & Hudson.

Danto, A. C. (1994). Embodied Meanings: Critical Essays and Aesthetic Meditations. New York: Farrar, Straus Giroux.

Davies, M. (2010). *The Corpus of Historical American English (COHA): 400 million words, 1810–2009*. www.english-corpora.org/coha/.

Davies, M. (2011). *Google Books Corpus. (Based on Google Books n-grams)*. www.english-corpora.org/googlebooks/.

Driver, F. (2001). *Geography Militant: Cultures of Exploration and Empire*. Oxford: Blackwell.

Driver, F. (2004). Distance and disturbance: Travel, exploration and knowledge in the nineteenth century. *Transactions of the Royal Historical Society, Sixth Series* 14, 73–92.

Efland, A. (1990). *A History of Art Education: Intellectual and Social Currents in Teaching the Visual Arts*. New York: Teachers College Press.

Egbert, J., Larsson, T. and Biber, D. (2020). *Doing Linguistics with a Corpus: Methodological Considerations for the Everyday User*. Cambridge: Cambridge University Press.

Elkins, J. (2009). On beyond research and new knowledge: Artists with PhDs. In J. Elkins (ed.), *On the New Doctoral Degree in Studio United States*. Washington, DC: New Academia Publishing, pp. 112–33.

Fairclough, N. (1992). *Discourse and Social Change*. Cambridge: Polity Press.

Flowerdew, J. (1996). Concordancing in language learning. In M. Pennington (ed.), *The Power of CALL*. Houston: Athelstan, pp. 97–113.

Garrett-Petts, W. F. and Nash, R. (2008). Re-visioning the visual: Making artistic inquiry visible. *Rhizomes* 18 (1). www.rhizomes.net/issue18/garrett/index.html.

Gibbons, J. (2007). *Contemporary Art and Memory: Images of Recollection and Remembrance.* London: I. B. Tauris.

Gillon, L. (2017). *The Uses of Reason in the Evaluation of Artworks: Commentaries on the Turner Prize.* London: Palgrave Macmillan.

Goldberg, R. (2001). *Performance Art: From Futurism to the Present.* New York: Thames & Hudson.

Gropius, W. (1965). *The New Architecture and the Bauhaus.* Cambridge, MA: MIT Press.

Halliwell, S. (1988). *Plato: Republic X.* Oxford: Oxbow Books.

Halpert, J. (2019, April 1). Interviews: Kameelah Janan Rasheed. *Artforum.* www.artforum.com/interviews/kameelah-janan-rasheed-talks-about-her-work-at-the-brooklyn-public-library-79129.

Harris, R. (2000). *Rethinking Writing.* London: Athlone Press.

Harris, R. (2003). *The Necessity of Artspeak: The Language of Arts in the Western Tradition.* London: Continuum.

Herman, O. and Kovář, V. (2013). Methods for Detection of Word Usage over Time. *Seventh Workshop on Recent Advances in Slavonic Natural Language Processing, RASLAN 2013.* Brno: Tribun, pp. 79–85.

Hocking, D. (2010). The discursive construction of creativity as work in a tertiary art and design environment. *Journal of Applied Linguistics and Professional Practice* 7 (2), 235–55.

Hocking, D. (2018). *Communicating Creativity: The Discursive Facilitation of Creative Activity in Arts.* London: Palgrave Macmillan.

Hocking, D. (2021). Artists' statements, 'how to guides' and the conceptualisation of creative practice. *English for Specific Purposes* 62, 103–16.

Hoey, M. (2005). *Lexical Priming: A New Theory of Words and Language.* London: Routledge.

Hunston, S. (2002). *Corpora in Applied Linguistics.* Cambridge: Cambridge University Press.

Huyssen, A. (2012). *Twilight Memories: Marking Time in a Culture of Amnesia.* New York: Routledge.

Itten, J. (1964). *Design and Form: The Basic Course at the Bauhaus.* London: Thames & Hudson.

Jansen, L., Luijten, H. and Bakker N. (eds.) (2009). *Vincent van Gogh: The Letters.* http://vangoghletters.org.

Johnson-Laird, P. N. (1988). Freedom and constraint in creativity. In R. J. Sternberg (ed.), *The Nature of Creativity: Contemporary Psychological Perspectives.* Cambridge: Cambridge University Press, pp. 202–19.

Kahnweiler, D. (1949). *The Rise of Cubism.* New York: Wittenborn, Schultz.

Kemmis, S. (2010). What is professional practice? Recognising and respecting diversity in understandings of practice. In C. Kanes (ed.), *Elaborating Professionalism: Studies in Practice and Theory*. London: Springer, pp. 139–65.

Kester, G. H. (2011). *The One and the Many: Contemporary Collaborative Art in a Global Context*. Durham, NC: Duke University Press.

Kilgarriff, A., Baisa, V., Bušta, J. et al. (2014). The Sketch Engine: Ten years on. *Lexicography ASIALEX* (1), 7–36.

Kilgarriff, A., Herman, O., Bušta, J., Rychlý P. and Jakubíček, M. (2015). *DIACRAN: A Framework for Diachronic Analysis*. www.sketchengine.eu/wp-content/uploads/Diacran_CL2015.pdf.

Klein, K. (2000). On the emergence of memory in historical discourse. *Representations* 69, 127–50.

Koester, A. (2010). Building a small specialised corpora. In A. O'Keeffe and M. McCarthy (eds.), *The Routledge Handbook of Corpus Linguistics*. Abingdon, UK: Routledge, pp. 66–79.

Lazzeretti, C. (2016). *The Language of Museum Communication: A Diachronic Perspective*. London: Palgrave Macmillan.

Leech, G. (2004). Recent grammatical change in English: Data, description, theory. In K. Aijmer and B. Altenberg (eds.), *Advances in Corpus Linguistics: Papers from the 23rd International Conference on English Language Research on Computerised Corpora (ICAME 23)*. Amsterdam: Rodopi, pp. 61–81.

Leech, G., Hundt, M., Mair, C. and Smith, N. (2009). *Change in Contemporary English: A Grammatical Study*. Cambridge: Cambridge University Press.

Lejeune, A., Mignon, O. and Pirenne, R. (2013). French theory and American art: An introduction. In A. Lejeune, O. Mignon and R. Pirenne, R. (eds.), *French Theory and American Art*. Berlin: Sternberg Press, pp. 9–41.

LeWitt, S. (1967, June). Paragraphs on conceptual art. *Artforum* 5(10), 79–83.

Liese, J. (2013). Toward a history (and future) of the artist statement. *Paper Monument* 4. https://nplusonemag.com/online-only/papermonument/toward-a-history-and-future-of-the-artist-statement/.

Marchi, A. (2018). Dividing up the data. In C. Taylor and A. Marchi (eds.), *Corpus Approaches to Discourse: A Critical Review*. London: Routledge, pp. 174–96.

Matisse, H. (1948). Exactitude is not truth. In H. Clifford (ed.), *Henri Matisse: Retrospective Exhibition of Paintings, Drawings and Sculpture*. Philadelphia: Philadelphia Museum of Art, pp. 33–4.

McEnery, T., Xiao, R. and Yukio, T. (2006). *Corpus-based Language Studies: An Advanced Resource Book*. New York: Routledge.

Miller, A. (2017). Creative geographies of ceramic artists: Knowledges and experiences of landscape, practices of art and skill, *Social & Cultural Geography* 18(2), 245–67.

Miskovic-Lukovic, M. (2009). Is there a chance that I might kinda sort of take you out to dinner? The role of the pragmatic particles kind of and sort of in utterance interpretation. *Journal of Pragmatics* 41(3), 602–25.

Nochlin, L. (1971). Why have there been no great women artists? *Art News* 69 (9), 22–39.

Ostrow, S. (2003, October 1). Sol LeWitt by Saul Ostrow. *Bomb 85*, 22–9. https://bombmagazine.org/articles/sol-lewitt/.

Parker, L. D., Jacobs, K. and Schmitz, J. (2019). New public management and the rise of public sector performance audit: Evidence from the Australian case. *Accounting, Auditing & Accountability Journal* 32 (1), 280–306.

Partington, A. (2010). Modern diachronic corpus-assisted discourse studies (MD-CADS) on UK newspapers: An overview of the project. *Corpora* 5 (2), 83–108.

Partington A., and Duguid, A. (2008). Modern diachronic corpus-assisted discourse studies (MD-CADS). In M. Bertuccelli-Papi and S. Bruti (eds.), *Threads in the Complex Fabric of Language: Linguistics and Literary Studies in Honour of Lavinia Merlini*. Pisa: Felici Editori, pp. 269–77.

Partington, A., Duguid, A. and Taylor, C. (2013). Modern diachronic corpus-assisted discourse studies (MD-CADS) 1: Comparisons over time in lexical grammar and discourse practices. In A. Partington, A. Duguid and C. Taylor (eds.), *Patterns and Meanings in Discourse: Theory and Practice in Corpus-assisted Discourse Studies (CADS)*. Amsterdam: John Benjamins Publishing Company, pp. 265–82.

Pennycook, A. (2007). 'The rotation gets thick. The constraints get thin': Creativity, recontextualisation and difference. *Applied Linguistics* 28 (4), 579–96.

Phillips, N. and Hardy, C. (2002). *Discourse Analysis: Investigating Processes of Social Construction*. Thousand Oaks, CA: Sage.

Quintilian, M. F. (1939). Institutio oratoria. In H. E. Butler (trans.), *The Institutio Oratoria of Quintilian*. London: William Heinemann. [Original work published AD 95.]

Rissanen, M. (2018). Three problems connected with the use of diachronic corpora. *ICAME Journal* 42, 9–12.

Robertson, J. and McDaniel, C. (2017). *Themes of Contemporary Art: Visual Art After 1980*. Oxford: Oxford University Press.

Roose, H., Roose, W., & Daenekindt, S. (2018). Trends in contemporary art discourse: Using topic models to analyze 25 years of professional art criticism. *Cultural Sociology* 12 (3), 303–324.

Rule, A. and Levine, D. (2012). International art English. *Triple Canopy* 16. www.canopycanopycanopy.com/contents/international_art_english.

Schmid, H. J. (2000). *English Abstract Nouns as Conceptual Shells*. Berlin: Mouton de Gruyter.

Schwarzenbach, J. and Hackett, P. (2015). *Transatlantic Reflections on the Practice-Based PhD in Fine Art*. Abingdon, UK: Taylor & Francis.

Seneca, L. A. (1925) Moral letters to Lucilius. In R. M. Gummere (trans.), *Ad Lucilium Epistulae Morales*. London: William Heinemann. [Original work published AD 65.]

Specht, S. M. (2010). Artists' statements can influence perceptions of artwork. *Empirical Studies of the Arts* 28 (2), 193–206.

Stanyer, J. and Mihelj, S. (2016). Taking time seriously? Theorizing and researching change in communication and media studies. *Journal of Communication* 66, 266–79.

Stein, J. (ed.). (1980). *The Bauhaus: Weimar, Dessau, Berlin, Chicago* (W. Jabs and B. Gilbert, trans.). Cambridge, MA: Massachusetts Institute of Technology.

Stokes, P. (2006). *Creativity from Constraints: The Psychology of Breakthrough*. New York: Springer

Sullivan, K. (2009). The languages of art: How representational and abstract painters conceptualize their work in terms of language. *Poetics Today* 30(3), 517–60.

Sweeney, J. J. (1946). *The Bulletin of the Museum of Modern Art XIII* (4–5), 19–21.

The Talks (2011, September) Gilbert & George: 'We don't do art for the few.' https://the-talks.com/interview/gilbert-george/.

Taylor, C. (2010). Science in the news. A diachronic perspective. *Corpora* 5(2), 221–50.

Temme, J. E. V. (1992). Amount and kind of information in museums: Its effects on visitors' satisfaction and appreciation of art. *Visual Arts Research* 18 (2), 28–36.

Trevelyan, J. (2013). *Peter McLeavey: The Life and Times of a New Zealand Art Dealer*. Wellington: Te Papa Press.

Vaughan, E. and Clancy, B. (2013). Small corpora and pragmatics. In J. Romero-Trillo (ed.), *Yearbook of Corpus Linguistics and Pragmatics*. London: Springer, pp. 53–73.

Walsh, S. (2013). Corpus linguistics and conversation analysis at the interface: Theoretical perspectives, practical outcomes. In J. Romero-Trillo (ed.), *Yearbook of Corpus Linguistics and Pragmatics*. London: Springer, pp. 37–51.

Wesner, S. (2018). *Artists' Voices in Cultural Policy: Careers, Myths and the Creative Profession after German Unification*. London: Springer.

Cambridge Elements ≡

Corpus Linguistics

Susan Hunston
University of Birmingham

Professor of English Language at the University of Birmingham, UK. She has been involved in Corpus Linguistics for many years and has written extensively on corpora, discourse, and the lexis-grammar interface. She is probably best known as the author of Corpora in Applied Linguistics (2002, Cambridge University Press). Susan is currently co-editor, with Carol Chapelle, of the Cambridge Applied Linguistics series.

Advisory Board

Professor Paul Baker, *Lancaster University*
Professor Jesse Egbert, *Northern Arizona University*
Professor Gaetanelle Gilquin, *Université Catholique de Louvain*

About the Series

Corpus Linguistics has grown to become part of the mainstream of Linguistics and Applied Linguistics, as well as being used as an adjunct to other forms of discourse analysis in a variety of fields. It continues to become increasingly complex, both in terms of the methods it uses and in relation to the theoretical concepts it engages with. The Cambridge Elements in Corpus Linguistics series has been designed to meet the needs of both students and researchers who need to keep up with this changing field. The series includes introductions to the main topic areas by experts in the field as well as accounts of the latest ideas and developments by leading researchers.

Cambridge Elements ≡

Corpus Linguistics

Elements in the series

Printed in the United States
by Baker & Taylor Publisher Services